Stay-At-Home
MOM$ MAKING
MONEY

7 Steps to Starting Your Own
Virtual Assistant Business

KAREN KAMENWA

Printed in the United States of America

ISBN: 978-0-692-82632-4

ADVANCE PRAISE

"The book does an excellent job of explaining what a virtual assistant business entails and is quite an easy read for someone starting their own business or for someone like myself who did not know what a virtual assistant does. The book provides readers with clear information on how to go about setting up a virtual assistance business, what resources exist for them, what to expect, and how to obtain and maintain clients. I have to say that while reading the book, I gained a thorough understanding of what a virtual assistant is. It also provides excellent information regarding customer service and servicing clients that could be used in any business or workplace."
— Angela Wheeler, Business Analyst

"Having been written from a firsthand perspective, this book offers easy to follow, step-by-step guidance on starting and running a virtual assistance business. I found the section on how to get new customers [to be] useful and critical, since finding clients is the lifeline of a young business. The book also discusses various online platforms that can be used to find clients. Overall, it is a relevant book to read and re-read from time to time to get useful reminders."

—Duncan Muguku, CEO and Founder, ThriveYard

"Great information! This is a well-written…guidebook on how to start and maintain a virtual assistance company. The book helps the reader learn how to avoid serious, expensive mistakes while equipping the person with vital information on how to start and maintain the business for the long haul.

Karen also equips the readers with tips on how to manage their emotional, mental, physical, and spiritual health. I like that she offers personal coaching after readers complete the book. A must-read."

—Veronica Gibbons, Registered Nurse

"A great, easy-to-read book. As a stay-at-home mom and virtual assistant, I found it to be very inspiring, relatable, and informative. I identified areas where I fall short as a virtual assistant and learned how to improve my services."

—Lydiah Ndung'u, Virtual Assistant

Dedication

To David and Charles, for always inspiring
me to be the best person that I can be.

I hope that you are inspired to seek, pursue,
and become who you were created to be.

TABLE OF CONTENTS

PART I

PART II

FOREWORD

By Anne Palmer, Author and Creator of
The Gifted Trap…EMERGE™ From Gifted to Great.

At birth we are each given an incredible opportunity. An opportunity to answer a call to use our gifts and make our lives meaningful by making a difference.

In my work as a clarity expert, author, speaker, and strategist, my purpose and passion is to empower organizations and high-achievers to *EMERGE*™ and *be great!* My mantra is: "To claim your greatness is not arrogant… To *not* claim it is!"

So, there are two vitally important questions I pose to you now: Do you listen? And are you answering your call?

This compelling and informative body of work, *Stay-at-Home Moms Making Money: 7 Steps to Starting Your Own Virtual Assistant Business,* is an excellent example of what it means to listen, answer, and ALIGN all that is asked of you in service to the world.

Karen Kamenwa has been an integral part of the success of my business—serving not just as my virtual assistant, but more as a vital partner and support system that allows me to align every aspect of what I am called to do. It brings me tremendous joy and pride to witness and testify to Karen's commitment to answer her call in service to others.

At its core, Karen's purpose is to enthusiastically acquire new knowledge and generously share relevant information that inspires and empowers others. She is living her purpose with this roadmap to success in business and in life for you!

Wherever you are on your journey to answer *your* call, this book is a must-read. It will open your eyes, and guide you as you create the professional and personal life you desire to have.

There are only two choices in life—to choose to do something, or to choose *not to do* something. Make the choice today to get busy reading *Stay-at-Home Moms Making Money: 7 Steps to Starting Your Own Virtual Assistant Business,* and applying the seven steps to ALIGN your life!

PART I

Introduction
WHEN DESTINY CALLS

When you have a sense of calling...there is something deep and enriching when you realize it isn't just a casual choice, it's a divine calling.
—Charles R. Swindoll

Hindsight is twenty-twenty. Have you ever experienced something in your life that you didn't quite understand at the time, but when you look back now, totally makes sense? Something that you now realize could not have gone any other way except the way it did? Well, I'm about to share with you one such experience.

When I started my virtual assistant business ten years ago, my very first client was an entrepreneur, book publisher, and author. She hired me as her virtual assistant because she had just self-published a book that had become an instant success. She could no longer keep up with the onslaught of emails from her readers, so she decided to hire me to help her respond to the hundreds she was receiving daily—that's what a virtual assistant does. Her role is to relieve the business owner of the workload that keeps her stuck in the day-to-day operations of her business, hindering her from focusing on revenue generating and business-growth activities that only she can perform.

While working with my first client, I learned that the reason she wrote and published books was to help her readers solve their problems using the information she provided in those books. I was very inspired by her generosity and desire to serve people in this way. What intrigued me was that solving people's problems was her livelihood. Her solutions were appreciated by customers who in turn generously expressed their gratitude by purchasing her books. It was a win-win, and that idea fascinated me.

Being me, I started thinking about all the knowledge I had acquired up until that point to see whether anyone could benefit from it. I got down to work, did a whole ton of research, and created an ebook draft. I was so pleased with myself. I felt excited and accomplished. Off I emailed my new creation—an ebook packed with a lot of valuable information, or so I thought—to my client for feedback. I candidly shared with her my hope to sell the ebook online, just like she did, and help many people. She reviewed my ebook and gave me her honest but painful feedback: She commended me for my hard work but told me straight up that the solutions I was offering in my ebook was not material that anyone would pay for.

Do you recall a time when you were giddy with excitement about something you had done, only to have your hopes dashed as soon as you shared it with someone? I was heartbroken and, to be honest, I felt a little stupid. My short-lived dream of becoming an author, of solving humanity's problems through a book, came to a screeching halt!

I quickly dropped the idea, shifted gears, and refocused my time and energy on what I knew how to do best. That was relieving my clients of time-consuming yet necessary back-office administrative tasks so that they could focus on their zone of genius: the things they enjoyed doing or that only they could do in their businesses. I did an excellent job as a virtual assistant, and my clients loved me for it. It brought me a great sense of joy and fulfillment to know that I was making a difference in my clients' businesses and in their lives. They had peace of mind knowing that they could trust me to complete the tasks assigned to me on time and that their businesses were growing and moving forward with ease.

RELENTLESSLY PURSUED

But the surprising thing that happened was that, although I dropped the idea of writing the ebook, every few months the idea would come back and interrupt my thoughts. I kept ignoring it. Over the coming year and a half, one thought recurred and became clearer and more defined. The thought was: *Write about what you do. Teach others about what you do.* I continued to ignore it and instead poured my heart and energy into what was in front of me, which was my virtual assistant business— that was what I had confidence in and enjoyed doing.

Has that ever happened to you? Has your spirit ever been crushed by someone you looked up to? Or have you even been discouraged by someone whose opinion mattered to you? That was me. The reason that I kept ignoring the constant reminders to write my book was because I doubted that I had anything valuable to share. I believed what my mentor-client had told me. After all, she was an expert! She was an author and a publisher. *She must be right,* I thought.

Then one day, about eighteen months after my initial ebook-writing attempt, I made the decision to write a book on how to start a virtual assistant business. I recall running the idea by my sister and my cousin, who were both working for me as virtual assistants at the time. They both thought it was a brilliant idea. We brainstormed relevant topics to include in the book, and off I went to work again. I buried myself in my computer, researching and writing. I was ready to make this dream happen. And then life happened!

Isn't it uncanny when you decide to do something significant in your life that a major life-changing event happens right around the same time? For example, a friend of mine recently decided to start her psychotherapy business. She signed a one-year lease to secure her office space, bought office furniture, and was ready to start scheduling clients when out of the blue, or so it seemed, her husband got offered a great job out of state. It turned out that her husband's old résumé was found online by his new employer, who invited him to an interview. To cut this long story short, he was offered the position, and the family had to relocate within less than two months. All of my friend's grand plans about opening her own psychotherapy office were derailed!

Well, around the time that I decided to write my book on how to start a virtual assistant business, I found myself in the throes of a custody battle for my kids. I got wrapped up in the emotional turmoil that ensued and was left with no mental or emotional capacity to take on the sacred incubation and birthing process of writing a book. So, I put the idea back on the shelf, so to speak, and turned all my energy and time to my kids and my business. I focused on being emotionally present for my children, taking care of their day-to-day needs, taking them to school, helping them with their homework, and preparing their meals, all while running my business, managing household chores, paying bills, and finding time to invest in my emotional healing during this traumatic season of our lives. The kids and I managed life as best as we could.

When the legal process came to an end, it left me emotionally exhausted and mentally drained. But there was hope. Thank God for hope! We were starting a new season, a new beginning. It was time to rebuild our lives.

Little by little, my kids and I started to heal. I was strengthening and rebuilding my inner self. I started volunteering at my local church: I ushered in congregants, printed bulletins, and ran the PowerPoint presentations for the worship songs and sermons. My healing continued to accelerate as I received prayer, love, and support from members of the congregation. I knew that I was on a good path, and I was optimistic. There was a bright light at the end of the dark tunnel. We were very close to it, and that motivated me to keep pushing forward toward being strong and healthy.

After some time, I started to relax. I started to breathe again. I started to enjoy my life again. Then that recurring thought came back to my mind again: *You need to write the book.* This time it really got my attention. I realized that this thought was never going to leave me until I acted upon it. This was now five years after I sent the first ebook draft to my book-publishing client. Five years down the road, and this relentless thought would not leave me alone! It was during this time that I remember listening to a sermon preached by T.D. Jakes, a famous American pastor, who said, "You know you are called to do something by God[1]* when that idea does not leave you, no matter how much time passes or how much you ignore it." It was at this moment that I realized that writing this book was a divine assignment, and that I needed to answer this call because it would never go away until I acted on it.

I decided to get serious. I wanted to be obedient to this call, now that I knew it was a God-given assignment. I wanted to get it done! Well, me being me, I jumped on it and decided to get this assignment done the quickest way possible. Without consulting the Giver of the assignment or finding out how He wanted the assignment executed, I delved into my archives and retrieved my initial notes from years before, when I had first done a brainstorming session with my sister and cousin. I created a new table of contents with relevant topics and embarked on a second research endeavor.

---

1   * Throughout this book I will refer to God and share some of my
    stories through the lens of my faith as a Christian, but this is by
    no means a religious book. The information and steps I teach on
    how to start your virtual assistant business are applicable regardless
    of your religious beliefs, ethnicity, race, background, culture, or
    economic or social status.

To be honest, I felt totally inadequate to take on this project. I had absolutely no idea what I was doing. I was clueless about how to get the assignment done, and so I decided to hire a ghostwriter. I gave him my table of contents and specific guidance regarding the information I wanted to be included in the book, along with the tone of voice that I wanted for the book, and I was all set. Two weeks later, my book was ready. I paid the guy. I had the ebook in my hands—well, on my computer. It was complete and ready for publishing, or so I thought!

As I read the hot-off-the-press book, something just didn't sit well with me. The book was just not *me*! It didn't sound like me at all! I didn't even like it! I embarked on an editing exercise that was more like an overhaul, just to bring my voice into the book. I might as well have written the whole book from scratch, because I changed almost all of it. Afterward, I felt much better about it. The book now had my signature voice and fingerprint. I shared it with a few of my trusted and generous friends and family for proofreading. They edited it and gave me their honest feedback. I will forever be grateful for the generosity, time, and effort they put into proofreading my book. (If you are reading this book, you know who you are—thank you!)

After incorporating all their edits and feedback, I was thrilled that the book was finally getting closer to publication. I came up with the title of the book, wrote my back-cover copy, and hired a graphic designer. I paid for an ISBN number, and I was ready to get the book published. My graphic designer created a beautiful cover and got it Amazon Kindle ready. The book was prepared to get into the hands of its readers, and I was finally going to complete my divine assignment.

PARALYZED BY FEAR AND DOUBT

It had taken me about six months to get the book to this place, yet I just could not get myself to upload it to the Amazon site. I was paralyzed by fear. I was overwhelmed with tremendous feelings of doubt. I started to question whether the book was really needed, and if it would really help anyone. I remember sharing these doubts with my cousin, who is also an author. He encouraged me with these wise words that I'll never forget: "If your book helps one person, it has done its job." That sentence inspired me to move past my doubt, because I was certain that my book could help at least one person. I had already received all the validation I could ever need from my family, my friends, and my editorial team, because not only could they not wait for the book to be published, they had lists of people that they intended to recommend the book to once it was available for purchase.

You would think that was enough to pull me out of my paralysis, right? Wrong! Fear and doubt continued to plague my mind. I was stuck. By the start of the new year, I had still not published my book. It was hiding in my computer, unpublished, and it was not serving anyone—certainly not the people it was supposed to help.

Now that several people had been involved in editing my book, and I had told a few more friends that I was writing it, I was really feeling the pressure! Every once in a while a friend or two would ask me when the book was going to be published or if I was done writing it. And since I didn't want them to think that I was a liar, I knew that I had to publish the book. I also had to remind myself that this was not an assignment I had given myself; it was a divine assignment. Talk about accountability!

I, being the kind of person who cares about my reputation and never wants to be known as a liar, have learned that the best way to accomplish my goals or dreams is to share them with at least three people. I encourage you to do the same. These three people will, by default, become your accountability partners. Every time you meet with them or talk to them, you will inadvertently remember the goals you shared with them, and you will invariably feel the pressure to accomplish them. Each time you meet them, you will want to be able to report positive progress about the dream you shared with them. Which means that they will be pushing you to manifest your dreams even without their realization. That kind of pressure is good because it motivates you to accomplish your goals.

DIVINELY ORCHESTRATED

Now, here's a twist to the story! At the end of every year, I come up with a theme for the upcoming new year. I have been doing this for at least five years now. The theme comes to me after prayer and meditation. My theme for the coming year at this time was rest. I felt that I was not to do any new or major projects either in my business or in ministry. I was to rest. It was a season to be nourished, fed, and replenished. I was to go on furlough. And so I had the perfect reason to let my book rest for the year. Anytime I attempted to pick up my book and start working on what was left to do to get it out to the world, I remembered that it was my year of rest and I was not to do anything with it.

And so I rested, and the year came and went. When it came to an end, during my prayer and meditation time, the new theme that I was given for 2018 was surrender. I felt that I was being asked to surrender and allow God to do His will in my life.

I had absolutely no idea what to expect, but I was refreshed, rejuvenated, and excited for the new things that were on the horizon. And as I started to plan what to focus on in the new year, the thought came to my mind again. This time it was: *You haven't completed your book yet.* I immediately knew that it was time to resume the book project; I knew that it was imperative that I do it! It was time to get it done!

This being my year of surrender, I surrendered to this mandate, to this calling, to this assignment to complete and publish the book. A few months into the new year, I had a very interesting dream. I was in a hospital delivery room waiting to give birth to my baby. I had no support, no family, no spouse, no friends, and no midwife with me. I was alone. My kids were waiting for me in the waiting room; they were not allowed in the delivery room because they were underage. There were several pregnant women in the delivery room. Each one had the support of loved ones: spouses, parents, siblings, children, or friends to encourage, support, and love them as they waited with eager anticipation for their newborn's arrival.

I asked three nurses for the whereabouts of my midwife and only one of them had an answer for me. She told me that my midwife was in New Zealand! I was alarmed! What was my midwife doing abroad? I wasn't in labor yet, but I must have been close since I was in the delivery room. Or maybe I had decided to check myself in early just to be prepared, since I didn't have the support of family or relatives. I don't know why, but all the same, I panicked. What if I went into labor and my midwife hadn't arrived yet? Then I suddenly woke up from my dream. I was still a little anxious, but after prayer and reflection, I realized that the dream was showing me that I was pregnant with my book and I was going to deliver it soon. However, I didn't have the support that I needed to birth this baby into the world.

I knew right then that I needed the right support to successfully usher this book into the world. In surrender, I asked God to provide the midwife and the support that I needed to deliver the baby.

A few months later, I was watching a particular YouTube video when an ad popped up. I was introduced to my midwife—Angela Lauria, my book mentor. She was the answer to my prayer. She and her team helped me birth this book and bring it into the world.

I tell you all this so that I can give you some background on why I wrote this book.

So why exactly *did* I write this book? I wrote it in response to God's calling. I wrote it because He assigned me this task and would not reassign it to anyone else. He reminded me of this assignment persistently. And so I responded. I wrote this book to answer God's calling.

Unbeknownst to me, the desire to write this book ten years ago was not a result of my own will or volition. Remember how I started this chapter? "Hindsight is twenty-twenty"? Yes, looking back in hindsight, now I know: God was orchestrating things all along. It was not a coincidence that my first client was an author and a publisher—God divinely connected me with my first client. He set me on the path that led me to be inspired by someone who had answered her calling. Although she discouraged me when I first wrote my ebook, she was put in my life to be an example and a model to emulate.

Can you relate? If you look back on your life, I'm sure you will find events that took place that are not coincidences—these events or people were instrumental in bringing you to where you are today. Even picking up this book and reading it is not a coincidence. God is divinely orchestrating and connecting you to the people and things you need along your life's journey to take you to your destiny.

Over time, God refined my desire and made it clear that I was to share the knowledge that I had acquired over the years, running my virtual assistant business as a stay-at-home-mom, so that other mothers desiring to do the same would have the opportunity to achieve similar results a lot faster and with much more ease by following the steps that I share in this book.

WHAT TO EXPECT

The book is divided into two parts. The first part focuses on preparing you to start your business. It's about getting clear about who you are, your core values, what you really want for yourself and your family, so that you can create a clear vision for your future. The second part of the book is where the rubber meets the road. This is where we lay down the foundation for your business, get it started, and learn how to sustain it while balancing your family life.

I will teach you my seven-step process, which I call the ALIGNED process. It is a blueprint that I developed through my entrepreneurial journey, which has been filled with many lessons, challenges, joys, growth, mistakes, successes, frustrations, tears, transformation, and laughter. I put all of my experience in a systematic process that is easy to follow and apply. This process will help you create a business that gives you the freedom and flexibility you need to uncompromisingly put your family first.

So, what *is* the ALIGNED process? The word "ALIGNED" is an acronym. Each letter in the word represents a step in the process. The steps are:

- **Step One: A – Assess Your Life.** This step is all about finding out what *you* really want.

- **Step Two: L – Look Within to Find Your Assets.** You will go on an exploratory journey to really get to know *you*. Who are you? What's your personality like? What's your love language? What's your temperament? What are your strengths? How about weaknesses? What are your gifts, talents, skills? You will get to know you, and you will be pleasantly surprised at what you discover!

- **Step Three: I – Ingest and Integrate.** Here we put together the information from steps one and two, create a simple business plan, and set goals for your business that are in alignment with your core values, goals, and priorities.

- **Step Four: G – Go! Get Your Business Started.** You will get all the information you need to understand the workings of a virtual assistant business: the skills, qualifications, and equipment you'll need, how to receive payments from clients, where to find clients, how to bid for jobs, how to market your business, how to work with your first client, how to grow and expand your business, and so much more.

- **Step Five: N – Nurture What You Create.** Here you will learn strategies to help you nurture a sustainable business that keeps growing and evolving.

- **Step Six: E – Embrace and Enjoy.** You will learn how to create balance, manage your time, set boundaries, and avoid stress, overwhelm, and burnout so that you can embrace and enjoy your mompreneur journey.

- **Step Seven: D – Dream and Grow.** You will learn about the opportunities available for growing and expanding your business and yourself. I will share with you the different opportunities for virtual assistants who want to maximize their gifts to fulfill their life's purpose.

You will also learn how to apply the ALIGNED process for every new dream you want to accomplish.

"IS THIS BOOK FOR ME?"

If you're contemplating leaving your full-time job to be a stay-at-home mom and you're scared to death about how you and her family will make ends meet, keep reading. This book is for you.

If your maternity leave is about to come to an end and you're anxious and worried sick at the thought of leaving your six-week-old baby with a stranger at a day care center, do not put this book down. Keep reading. It's for you!

If you're trapped in a situation or a circumstance that you don't want to be in because your inability to make a financial contribution in your home affects your ability to stand up for yourself or makes you feel voiceless or powerless, this book is for you. This book will show you that you have what it takes to be financially empowered, be an amazing mom, and have a voice.

If you feel powerless and stuck in an abusive relationship because you believe that you can't make it on your own, keep reading. This book is for you. You have so many gifts and talents, abilities, strengths, and skills that are locked inside of you waiting to be unleashed!

If you know that you have so much to offer the world but don't know how to monetize your gifts and talents, read on, because this book is for you.

If you know that being an extraordinary stay-at-home mom and wife is what you desire, yet something inside of you tells you that there's more for you to do, that you are capable of much more. This book is for you!

If the thought of dying having not accomplished all that you know you are called to do on this earth petrifies you, this book is for you.

If your marriage is falling apart and you hope that making a financial contribution to your household budget will relieve your partner's stress and improve your relationship, this book is for you.

If you are dying inside, clueless about the untapped potential and greatness locked inside of you, this book is for you.

If you know that starting your virtual assistant business is what you need to do, and you know it's time to do it, but you don't have the support that you need to make it a reality, this book is for you.

This book is for you because you want to make the contribution and the difference you were born to make on this planet and in your generation.

My prayer is that one day in the future you will look back in hindsight and realize that reading this book was not a coincidence but was divinely orchestrated to inspire you and propel you toward your destiny.

CHAPTER 1
A LIFE-CHANGING EVENT

"Your life will never be the same!" If there's anything that I was told over and over again during my first pregnancy, it was these seven words. I found it very hard to grasp what those words really meant. I had seen so many pregnant women have babies, and I had never observed any drastic changes in their lives apart from the new, cute little addition, of course. These bundles of joy were often adorable when nice, quiet, and happy, but total nightmares when unhappy, wet, or hungry. That was normal. That was to be expected. It came with the territory, right? I also guessed that a new baby must come with a huge financial responsibility, but since everyone, rich or poor, seemed to be getting babies, I figured it couldn't be that bad. What I couldn't figure out was why every parent, seasoned or not, had the same words of wisdom to share. They didn't say it in the exact same way, but they basically meant the same thing: "Enjoy your life now, because it's about to change forever!"

Well, I was excited to be pregnant with my first baby, and I waited with such eager anticipation to meet my son that nothing could have dampened my spirit or deterred me from devouring every parenting magazine and online article I found to help me prepare for his coming. I wanted to be the best mom that I could be, and I wanted to know what to expect when he made his grand entrance.

But true to their words, the day did come when I completely understood what they'd all meant when they said that my life would never be the same again. Twelve years into motherhood and two kids in tow, I have caught myself giving the same advice to first-time moms: "Sleep as much as you can now. Your life will never be the same again!"

It's so true. Life really does change once you become a mother: round the clock, day in, day out, from nursing, changing diapers, pureeing food, playing peek-a-boo, and doctor's visits; to school field trips, soccer games, school plays, dental appointments, emergency room trips, and homework; you name it. You get to experience it all. It's the adventure of a lifetime. You never know what's coming. You just buckle your seat belt and enjoy the roller coaster ride.

A CATALYST FOR CHANGE

And that's not the only change that takes place once you become a mom. Motherhood is a catalyst for so many changes in your life that, truly, nothing is ever the same again. It's almost as though once the baby is born, a series of unexpected and uncontrollable chain reactions begins to take place, a transformation not only in your physical body but also in your way of thinking and your way of being. I believe that some of your untapped abilities, locked inside of you before giving birth, are unlocked after you become a mom.

Did you ever play house or pretend? Remember how you took care of your dolls, fed and dressed them? You talked to your dolls, taught them, cooked and had tea parties with them, right? Unbeknownst to you, you were preparing for motherhood. That nurturing instinct that no one taught you, that natural thing in you that drew you to dolls and to playing house, was a glimpse of the potential that was locked inside you. This gift is in every little girl waiting to be fully expressed when she first becomes a mother. It's a miracle, it's special, and it's beautiful. It's an experience that's so unique that no two mothers share the same exact experience or express it in the same way, yet it's so similar that all mothers can relate and connect to each other's nurturing instinct and experience. Now, isn't that something!

How about creativity? Do you remember how creative you were when you were a little girl? It didn't take much to get imaginative and creative. Drawing pretty flowers and rainbows, making rag dolls, knitting little sweaters, sewing doll clothes, making bead necklaces and rubber band bracelets, holiday decorations and ornaments—it all came so easily. I believe that you were practicing for your future because your creativity valve got turned on at full strength with the arrival of your first baby.

I cannot count how many times I have been super mom and saved the day for my kids. Whether it's braiding hair or taping a shoelace that has come undone and can't fit in the eyelet of a shoe, helping your seven-year-old create a diorama for school, or frantically making a last-minute Halloween costume, I know for sure that your creativity has been put to test numerous times. It still baffles me that teachers assign school projects to elementary school kids knowing full well that there's absolutely no way the kids could do them without a parent's help. I have yet to understand how teachers actually think that your seven- or eight-year-old can build half the things that they ask them to build for their school projects. It's still a mystery to me, but to keep my sanity, I concocted a conspiracy theory: I think teachers and God are in collaboration to get your creativity flowing at full capacity! Why else would they send your kids home to do science projects with a list of instructions and materials, half of which you've never heard of? You understand what I am saying?

On a serious note though, have you thought about your resourcefulness? Since you were a little girl, you somehow knew how to make things better, prettier, unique, or more special. Perhaps it was the words you spoke that made everything better, your special touch that calmed everyone down, or your smile that lit up the room. Maybe it was your presence, kindness, gentleness, graciousness, wit, or charm, that special something that you did naturally that seemed to change everything around you. It was that quality in you that made the difference—you had this knack for creating new things or making things different or better with your own unique touch. Who knew that you would need it when you needed to transform leftovers into a delicious meal that had everyone begging for more? Who knew that your ability to stretch the dollars would one day be the gift that enabled you to buy everything your family needed? It's nothing short of a miracle!

UNIQUELY GIFTED

What makes you uniquely you?

Since I was little, I quietly observed my environment, especially during a crisis. I was able to instinctively sense and discern what was needed. And I always made myself useful and became who I needed to be in order to help in that situation.

I recall a time when my brother fell sick in the middle of the night. He caused a huge commotion as he fell in the hallway and woke us all up. As you would imagine, we were all worried and concerned about his health. We didn't know what had caused him to pass out. My dad, who typically didn't seem to be able to handle these types of stress well, started humming songs that sounded like dirges! That didn't help the situation at all. In that moment, I quickly assessed the situation and the atmosphere, and I sensed that my mom needed us to be strong and helpful. She sent all my crying siblings back to their bedrooms, and only those who were strong stayed. I stayed and was ready to be put to work to do whatever Mom needed me to do to take care of my brother.

I have been and continue to be in many situations that call for me to assess the needs of a given situation, then step up to be a part of the solution whenever I can. It's not until I became a mom though that I realized that it was a gift. The gift that I'd had since I was a little girl has now grown. I am very sensitive to my environment, and my ability to recognize unspoken needs has proven to be a very useful skill as a mother and also in daily interactions with other people. Even when it's as subtle as a slight inflection of someone's voice, a fleeting facial expression, or any other body language, I'm able to understand the nonverbal communication whether it's expressed out loud or not. And I need it with my boys. When they tell me one thing but they really mean another, I'm able to creatively get to the heart of the matter and address some of their unspoken concerns directly or indirectly, regardless of whether they voice them or not, because I'm able to sense them.

How about your life-giving ability? We were created with the ability to bring forth life. There's no greater or more powerful evidence that mothers are life-giving beings than the living children we bear. And once you become a mom, your life-giving nature is amplified! Your ability to give life to your environment, to your relationships, and to your work increases dramatically, and it's up to you to truly own this power for good. We have the ability to bring positive life into everything we do and touch.

Erick S. Gray captures this concept so perfectly in his quote: "Whatever you give a woman, she will make greater. If you give her a sperm, she'll give you a baby. If you give her a house, she will give you a home. If you give her groceries, she will give you a meal. If you give her a smile, she'll give you her heart. She multiplies and enlarges what's given to her."

If your mind used to race at a hundred miles an hour before you were pregnant with your first child, I'm sure it's now racing even faster: so many creative ideas, so many worries, so many concerns, possibilities, fears, worries, dreams, and goals for yourself and for your family.

It's no wonder that you're considering starting your virtual assistant business. Your creative nature wants to create a solution that will honor your life-giving, creative, and nurturing qualities so that you can be the best mom that you can be for your family while creating and designing a lifestyle that honors who you are and what you desire for your family through your business.

PREPARED FOR YOUR JOURNEY

You've been preparing for this moment from the day you were born. You've been creating, nurturing, and giving life all along, and now the moment has come to give life again. It's time to create and to nurture again. It's time bring to life your virtual assistant business. It calls for the same abilities that you know are not only innate but that you've been putting into practice all your life.

Just like giving birth to your first child is a life-changing event, starting your virtual assistant business is yet another life-changing event! But you are already well prepared for this event, because you are a mom!

Many of the skills you apply in motherhood and managing your household will come in handy in your business. However, please be warned that when you will never be 100 percent confident that you are making the right decision. You have to take a leap of faith because fear and doubt will show up at your doorstep as soon as you decide that you want to embark on this journey. I can guarantee you that.

You will be afraid of not only failing but also of being successful, just the same way you doubted that you could be a good mom while you were pregnant. Does that fear or doubt stop you from waking every morning and trying to be the best mom that you can be? No. You still love your kids and take care of them. And even right now, can you say that you have zero fear or anxiety about your kids and whether they will turn out okay? I'm sure your answer is no, but you still do the best you can.

The same will be true in your business. Every day from the moment you decide to start your own business, you will experience fear and doubt. It's normal. You may doubt that you will get a paying client; you may fear that you don't have the right skills or the right business acumen. Trust me, this is normal. In fact, I recently told one of my coaching clients that I would be concerned if she wasn't experiencing feelings of doubt or fear as she sets out to start her business. Fear is evidence that we desire to succeed. So, it's a good thing. If you really didn't care whether you succeed or not, there would be no reason to be anxious or fearful. Right?

Every time we step into something new or up to our next level, we are met with resistance to test our resolve. The way to push past the fear and doubt is to keep moving forward by taking the necessary steps to accomplish your dream. It will take courage. Courage is doing it anyway, despite the fear or doubt.

Trust me when I tell you that you've already accomplished great things in your life that caused you to push past even greater fears. Being a mom is not for the faint of heart, and here you are doing it every single day! So keep pushing forward and don't quit!

In the next chapter, I will share the raw yet real thoughts that tormented me right after I had my first child. As a first-time mom who was contemplating going back to work after maternity leave, the idea of a total stranger raising my child in a daycare center was excruciatingly painful. I wanted to be a wonderful mom and I always wanted to be there for my son. I felt taking him to a daycare facility would be a case of letting my son down. That thought alone made me feel very guilty.

Yet those feelings of guilt and my desire to be the best mom that I could propel me to start my virtual assistant business.

CHAPTER 2
JOLTED BACK TO REALITY

"Courage is the most important of all the virtues because without courage, you can't practice any other virtue consistently."
—*Maya Angelou*

I remember as if it was yesterday when we welcomed my firstborn son home from the hospital. The joy I felt was indescribable. I was filled with awe and wonder at my whole birthing experience. Nothing prepared me for the flood of love that filled my heart when I held my baby boy in my arms for the first time. It was an incredible feeling. This tiny little human had come out of my body! With all his body parts, ten tiny toes and fingers, all intact! It was nothing short of a miracle! I was in a constant state of amazement. I recall nursing him to sleep and holding him for hours on end, staring at my newborn baby, captivated by his beauty and peacefulness as he slept. *Truly, there must be a God,* I thought. If ever I had had any doubts, my firstborn son dispelled that thought from my mind completely.

The days and weeks of my maternity leave passed like a blur. It was as if I was caught in a time bubble where time literally stopped. Nights and days seemed to merge into one another as my son settled into his sleeping pattern while I was almost entranced, totally mesmerized by my new love. My purpose for existence at that point in time seemed to be to feed him, change his diapers, bathe him, hold him and stare into his little face for hours in fascination.

It was not until the day I received a phone call from my sister that I was jolted back to reality! As was characteristic of our conversations, she asked me what I was doing, and I told her the exact same thing that I had a few days prior to that, and a couple more days prior to that: "I'm just holding the baby and staring at him."

And she replied, "You know you'll have to get back to real life, right?" There was something about how she said those words, or maybe it was the tone of her voice that burst my magical bubble! It was as if I had taken a trip to the moon, then suddenly I was falling back to planet Earth, accelerating back to reality with the alarming force of gravity, and boom! My fairy tale was over. And for the very first time it hit me that I was a mom! I had a baby! I had responsibilities! There was life after the baby comes home!

YOU WILL NEVER BE FULLY READY

Just like that, my mind started flooding with worrisome thoughts. *Will I be a good mom? Can I be a good mom? Do I have what it takes? Will I love my baby well? What if I can't take care of him? What if we can't afford to provide everything that the baby needs? What if he falls sick?* And on and on these thoughts kept coming.

Do you remember your experience when you brought your first baby home from the hospital? What was your experience like?

That is one thing that no one prepares us for! All the well-meaning, unsolicited-advice-giving moms forgot to tell us this one thing: When you become a mom, you sign up for a lifetime of worrying about your kids' well being. You constantly doubt God's wisdom in entrusting you with the responsibility of motherhood. If you are like me, you had no clue what you signed up for, or did you? I think it was all written in fine print, just above the signature line—you know the small print that no one reads? Yep, that's where they tacked in that sentence (pun intended)!

All that aside, the joy, heartache, pain, laughter, pulled heartstrings, and sweet, memorable moments make motherhood well worth it, because many of us are not content with just one munchkin, we go back for a second helping, and a third, a fourth, a fifth, and even more… Kind of like an all-you-can-eat buffet. We don't stop until we say it's enough!

But this worrying thing, it just never stops! It's like a cloud that hangs over you twenty-four hours a day, seven days a week, and won't go away. Sometimes it's a real dark, low-hanging cloud that threatens to burst, and other times it's a few scattered clouds on the far horizon. I get it. Being halfway through your maternity leave makes it even worse, because you still haven't figured out childcare.

Remember the well-wishing, experienced moms who gave you advice when you were pregnant? They told you to stock up on your sleep because once the baby came, you would be up most of the night nursing the baby and changing diapers. To this day, I still haven't figured that out. How do you store sleep in advance? That's still a mystery to me, because they didn't loop me in on that secret. Did they share it with you? I would love to know.

What they also didn't say is that part of your sleep deprivation will arise from worrying yourself sick about the imminent end of your maternity leave.

In the dead of the night, as the baby nurses and drifts off to sleep, your mind is wide-awake from the relentless onslaught of thoughts…

Countdown: four more weeks to the first day back to work from maternity leave. Oh no, work! I wonder what they are up to and if they did finally launch the new products that they were planning to. Hmmm, I wonder if Naomi was able to transition well after I left... No one called me; I guess everything's going okay. Wow, I can't imagine going back to the same routine, doing the same things over and over again, being around the same people all day... I don't know, it seems like another world from a distant time. I really don't want to go back to work.

Who will babysit the baby when I go back to work? Hub can't help me; he has to work full time and his business is not doing so well. We need my income. But really, do I have to go back to work? What will happen if I don't? But I can't afford not to work. We need the money. We have a mortgage that we can't afford! Why did we buy this home? It's stretching us too thin.

I can't take the baby to daycare! He could never make it there; it will be too traumatizing. No! That's not an option! Maybe I should quit my job. Maybe it's really time for me to start my virtual assistant business. I really think it's what I need to do. But businesses take so long to start making money. What if I fail? A sigh... Hub will never agree to that; he has been against the idea since the first time I mentioned it to him.

I hate the tension between us. I don't know what it is this time, because he is not even talking to me. This is not the right time to bring up this subject again. I understand that he has a lot of pressure, working hard and everything, and with the baby, he probably feels the pressure even more. Aaargggh! I hate these money problems. There just never seems to be enough.

I'm not going to think about the horror stories I have heard about kids being neglected in daycares. Little infants crying unattended for twenty or thirty minutes, or staying in soiled diapers for hours on end, not being fed on schedule, missing medications, workers forgetting the foods the kids are allergic to. I don't know how other moms are able to do this. What am I going to do? I just can't send the baby off to some strangers to watch him! He will be just one of the countless kids in the daycare and they won't care about him. There has to be a way!

MOM-GUILT

You have every right to be concerned about your baby's care after you return to work. The daycare problem is real. I had the unfortunate experience of arriving to pick up my son from a family daycare that we had enrolled him in, only to find a huge CLOSED sign from the Department of Social Services on the front door of the building. The family daycare's doors had been shut not too long before I arrived. The inspection report stated that the facility was unsafe! I was horrified and angry.

Angry at the owner of the daycare for putting my son in danger. Angry at myself for not having a supernatural ability to know that the facility was unsafe. Needless to say, I hugged my son and left feeling like the worst mom in the world.

And then there was the other time when I left my son with a different childcare provider, whom I found online. She had great Google reviews. She seemed kind, loving, and caring. She had a nice home and only two other kids at that time. I thought this would be the perfect solution. As I was driving off to work after dropping my son off with her, I had a "feeling like the worst mom" moment. You know that feeling you get when you leave your son screaming at the top of his lungs because of separation anxiety? Yep, I know you know what I'm talking about. I got to work feeling like the worst mom in this world. Somehow I made it through the day, said countless prayers, and hoped that my son was able to settle in, stop crying, and warm up to the babysitter. Evening came, and off I rushed to pick up my son. Then I got the most unexpected yet dreadful news: "Sorry, I can't watch your child. He cries too much!"

I was thinking, *What? Isn't that what childcare providers do? Console crying babies?* I was dumbfounded and speechless. Without a babysitter to take care of my son the following day, I was back to the drawing board again. I am sure you can relate.

How about going to work late for the nth time and dealing with a boss who is not understanding at all? Have you ever been up all night because your baby has a fever from teething, or from the flu, or from a running stomach, or from an allergic reaction to something he ate, and now you're afraid that you're going to lose your job because they can only work with you for so long? Your coworkers have even started giving you that side look because they always do your share of work when you miss work or come in late or leave early for doctor's appointments. You are constantly worried that you'll be the first one on the layoff list should they decide to downsize the company.

I have so many stories that I can share, and I know you do too.

And then there's the mortgage and the ever-increasing baby expenses.

One thing that I must pat my mommy-advisers' backs for is warning me about the crazy cost of diapers and formula. It made sense that these would be ongoing expenses for a while, and I could see why. What I didn't know is how fast you run out of diapers and formula, especially when you never get your baby to latch properly and have to depend on formula!

Talking about expenses, what about baby clothes? Did it occur to you that some of the cutest clothes you bought or received as gifts would never be worn by your baby? I mean, did you know that seasons would change before your son was old enough to fit some clothes, and when he was big enough to fit in them, they were no longer appropriate for the season? I mean, you can't dress your child in a fleece winter jumpsuit in the summer, no matter how cute and adorable he would look in it. Right?

And then of course there are the regular utility bills, mortgage, taxes, HOA fees, credit card payments, and if, God forbid, the baby ends up in daycare, you could easily be working to transfer your pay to your childcare provider.

If you're like me and you know that you want to have more than one child, know that unless you solve this problem once and for all, your kids will end up in daycare. If that's the last thing that you want to happen, then do something about it. I don't want you to go through the guilt of dropping off your baby to a stranger at a daycare facility and feeling miserable all the way to work, then worrying yourself sick all day wondering if he has been left unattended or is sitting in soiled diapers for hours.

I know you want to be the first person to see him smile, crawl, take his first step, and say "mama" or "dada" for the first time. You don't want to miss those once-in-a-lifetime moments and milestones that you will never get back. I want you to be there to capture those memories on video and in pictures.

That's the reason I wrote this book. I want to invite you to consider starting your virtual assistant business using the skills that you currently have to solve the financial problem that would result if you chose to stay at home and raise your kids without a plan for making income.

In the next chapter, you will learn exactly how starting my company helped me take care of this issue once and for all. The company I created gave me the freedom and flexibility to be present and available for my kids, to capture every milestone, to take care of them when they were unwell, and as they continue to grow older, to attend school trips, performances, and award ceremonies, help them with their homework and school projects, and much more. I am able to do things with my kids that are practically impossible to do when you are tied to a regular nine-to-five job. And you can be too.

CHAPTER 3
THERE MUST BE MORE TO LIFE...

"Without a purpose, life is motion without meaning, activity without direction, events without reason."
—Rick Warren

Countless times, my sister-in-law and I would chat for long hours on the phone, both dissatisfied with our lives, both believing that there must be more to life than what we had. For me, the sense of dissatisfaction was like that nauseating feeling you get in your first trimester. It lingers in the background, and there's no remedy. You learn to deal with it until it stops in the next trimester—if you're lucky.

Everything in my life looked great from the outside, but from the inside, it was falling apart. We had just bought our first home, my partner's business was not doing well, and the economy was steadily heading toward recession. Unbeknownst to everyone too was that my relationship with my partner was in shambles. I was experiencing the joy of motherhood and the pain of heartbreak all at the same time. I was so happy; my son filled me with joy. We were even blessed to have my mom living with us; she came to help us with the baby so that I could go back to work after maternity leave. Yet every day I would wake up, plaster a smile on my face, and pretend that I was happy, that everything was okay. Yet I was actually dying inside. Have you ever had such an experience? Have you worn a smile on your face, acted like everything was okay while knowing full well that your life was a mess?

It was during this time that I earnestly started searching for ways that I could make money from home. I knew that I didn't have too much time to figure it out: With only eight weeks of maternity leave, the time would go fast. So I began looking for creative ways to make an income without spending too much time on the business so that I could spend more time with my family.

My first idea was to create a seniors' health care classifieds website where home–health care agencies, assisted living homes, nursing homes, and other medical-related services and products would be listed and advertised. I quickly realized that it would be way too time-consuming, and it would also take a while before I started generating a decent income from it.

Next, I explored making cloth diapers to sell online. I did a ton of research, but it didn't seem to be the right idea. It just didn't resonate with me. I quickly abandoned the idea.

Then I decided to look at my skills, my experience, my gifts and talents and areas that I felt were my strengths. I researched the types of entrepreneurs who had my skillset and the services that they offered. And that is when I discovered virtual assistance. The more I learned about virtual assistance, the more excited I got. A spark was ignited inside of me, a ray of hope! I already had most of the basic skills that were needed to start a virtual assistant business: I was working as a head customer service representative at the time, I had office-administration experience, I loved to learn and research, and I was generally tech savvy. It became very apparent to me that virtual assistance was something that I would not only be skilled at, I was also excited about the prospect of doing it. The thing that attracted me the most though was that I could work from home. And that translated to me being a stay-at-home mom because I really wanted to raise my son.

How about you? What skills do you have? What experience, talents, or education background do you have? In Chapter Five, I'll go deeper on how to identify your gifts, talents, skills, education, and experience so that you can pinpoint the services that you could potentially offer your clients. But first, I want to share with you the mental struggle and challenges I faced before I started my business.

Now that I had my brilliant business idea, you would think that I would have quit my job and started my business. No. I was pregnant with our second child. I was very excited to have a second baby; my son would have a sibling and a playmate. And this time around, the pregnancy was different: I knew what to expect. I was a pro. But the joy and excitement came mixed with increased stress: Mom was no longer with us. My employer was downsizing in phases. We were really straining financially and on the brink of losing our home. And our relationship continued to be stressed. We still put on smiley faces and pretended that all was well, yet inside we were really struggling.

We were able to creatively figure out childcare for our kids. My partner and I worked around our schedules for a season. We also had a few live-in nannies for a period of time, but nothing was ever really satisfactory. Although it was convenient to have live-in nannies, having a stranger living in our home came with its own set of challenges—we lost our privacy and we never felt truly relaxed in our home with a stranger sharing our space. So for me, none of those solutions really worked. The same nauseating feeling of dissatisfaction returned again, and thoughts of starting my virtual assistant business reemerged.

I wish I could tell you that with the resurgence of these thoughts, I decided that enough was enough with the nannies, financial stress, and everything else that wasn't working in my life. I wish I could tell you that I decided to do something to change my situation. I didn't. I continued to show up day after day to a job that I no longer enjoyed, a job that I dreaded because I never knew when I would be summoned to my boss's office to receive my termination letter.

The dreadful day did come when I got laid off. It was part of the inevitable downsizing that resulted from the company outsourcing its manufacturing department to China. I saw it coming. Having already survived three layoff phases in two years, I had a foreboding sense that I would not make it through the next cut.

The Sunday before I was laid off, I went to church as usual. This was in November 2008 when the economic crisis was at its worst. The sermon was on God's provision in difficult economic times. An invitation was made to all those who were struggling financially to go up to the front of the church. I walked up to the altar along with others in the congregation. We were anointed with oil, hands were laid on us, and we received prayer.

Looking back, that was the beginning of a turning point of my life. I showed up to work the following Monday and, as God would have it, I was laid off. But I felt an overwhelming peace come over me. I was filled with gratitude for my employer and their kindness despite being laid off. I felt light and free! A new chapter of my life was beginning. I was finally at liberty to try my virtual assistant business. I had nothing to lose. The thing I was afraid of letting go of—the job that I had grown to dislike—was no longer mine!

I promised myself that before I looked for another job, I would first try out the business. If it failed, I would go search for a job.

Hopefully *you* won't wait till you are laid off to start your business. I know that you are gifted and talented, and what you bring to the table is a valuable business opportunity and the key to your freedom as a mother.

It's been ten years, as of the time of writing this book, since I started my virtual assistant business. I have never looked back. This is one of the best decisions that I have ever made in my life.

A GIFT THAT KEEPS ON GIVING

My virtual assistant business has become a gift that keeps on giving. I am able to design a lifestyle that I can afford for my family. I am able to be the mom that I've always wanted to be. I am available for my kids when they need me. I can plan my time around my kids' needs and schedules. Now that they are in school, I am able to pick them up from school and help them with their homework. I attend their school performances and award ceremonies. I can scale down my workload during summer break to spend quality time with my kids. These are blessings that I don't take for granted.

My business enables me to earn significantly more money that I did when I was employed. I am able to do things that I would never have been able to do at my previous job: I can afford to take days off as I need to, go on vacations and camping trips, travel for business, attend workshops and trainings, dedicate time for self-care, and give my time and money to my church, community, and charity organizations whose causes I believe in. I am also completely debt free.

I started as a solopreneur, but as of the time of writing this book, my business has a dedicated team of fifteen virtual assistants. It is a tremendous honor to be a channel that God uses to provide for my team and their families. Knowing that families are fed because of my decision to start my business humbles me. Little did I know that God had great plans on that one Sunday when I meekly walked down the aisle to the altar at my church to receive prayer. God had planned to provide not only for me and my family, but for families in six different countries as well.

The most fun part of my workday is serving my clients. I enjoy using my skills, gifts, and talents to make a difference in my clients' lives and businesses. I get to learn about and understand so many different types of businesses and how they work. And I get to know and have great relationships with amazingly gifted entrepreneurs. Nothing makes the time I spend working with my clients more worthwhile than knowing that I make a valuable contribution that's appreciated.

I think back to the many times, years before I started my business, when I thought that there must be more to life. My company is evidence that, truly, there is more. It's not just the business. It's the freedom, money, and meaning that it gives me so that I can design and live my life as I choose.

If there was one thing I could have done differently, I wouldn't have waited so long to start my business.

I say all this not to brag, but to encourage and inspire you. Because if I could do it, you can definitely do it too!

I mentioned briefly in the introduction the seven-step ALIGNED process that I developed as a result of almost ten years of experience running my virtual assistant business. In the next chapter, I will define each step in more detail, so stay with me.

CHAPTER 4
THE ALIGNED PROCESS

"When your values are clear to you, making decisions becomes easier."
—Roy E. Disney

Little did I know that getting laid off was a blessing in disguise. Looking back, I see that God was setting me up to start my business. With no job, I had nothing to lose. It was the perfect time to start my business.

And there began my journey. I didn't really know much—just the basics: I needed to register my business and find my first client. I had a computer with high-speed Internet and a phone, and that was enough to get me started.

Three weeks after registering my business, I got my first client. I was so elated! I instantly knew that my business idea was valid—one person was willing to pay for my services. Two months later, I got my second client, and about six or so months later, my third. My business was growing fast, and it was exhilarating. I was doing the work that I loved, enjoying my new adventure, working from home while spending more time with my kids. I was excited to have found clients and to be busy making money within just a few weeks of starting my business.

What I didn't anticipate was the long hours I would work, including weekends. I was so excited to get work done and to please my clients that I didn't set any boundaries to designate my work hours separately from my personal and family hours. Before I knew it, I had my kids enrolled in a daycare part time so that I could work while they were away. That was not in alignment with one of my main reasons for starting my business in the first place. But it wasn't until several years had passed that I learned how to structure my business to support my personal goals.

Over time, I also realized that I wasn't clear in my mind about my values and what I stood for. I accepted any client whose needs matched my skillset. I eventually learned that I could not serve my clients effectively if what they stood for or the services that they provided were against my own personal belief system. I once had to let go of a good client after working together for two years because I had to come to terms with the fact that through serving as his virtual assistant, I was promoting a cause that I did not agree with—it went against my personal ethics. I did not want to compromise my values and beliefs for the sake of money, so I had to let go of the client. I did it graciously, and my client was very understanding. In the process though I learned the importance of understanding your client's business and what they stand for *before* entering into a business relationship with them.

I also discovered over the years that I brought a lot more to the table than just my skills. My personality, my love language, my temperament, my gifts and talents, strengths and weaknesses were all part of the sum total of what I offered my clients. Being able to identify these qualities, leverage them in my business, and show up fully aware of who I am as a person and what I bring to the table changed how I interacted with my clients, how I presented myself and my services. This made my work more purposeful, meaningful, and fulfilling.

Beyond serving my clients, I learned how to develop client relationships built on trust and reliability, as well as how to add value to my clients' personal lives and their businesses. I learned how to become an indispensable, highly sought-out virtual assistant.

I learned how to take care of myself so that I could be healthy and strong spiritually, emotionally, mentally, and physically. I realized that working long hours behind your computer desk without intentionally taking breaks or designing a plan to incorporate physical activity could be disastrous for your health.

INSPIRED BY BOREDOM AND RESTLESSNESS

Seven years into my business, the company was running smoothly and I had a team of reliable and experienced virtual assistants working. It was then that I started to get bored and restless. The powerful, creative, life-giving part of me was looking for an outlet for the next new dream, the next adventure, or the next level of growth. I learned that it took courage to choose to pursue new dreams and goals, and to seek to grow perpetually.

Boredom and restlessness inspire creativity. It was during this time that I started contemplating everything that I had I learned in my business and started putting together the beginnings of what later on became my step-by-step blueprint that I call ALIGNED process. It is a systematic approach to help you get the best of two worlds: Be the amazing stay-at-home mom that you want to be, and create a successful virtual assistant business that supports your personal and family values.

The process is the sum total of over fifteen years of my business experience, tenof which are in running a virtual assistant business; thousands of dollars and hours invested in training programs and workshops; years of doing deep personal-growth work; priceless knowledge gleaned from successful entrepreneurs, mentors, and coaches that I've worked closely with; and hard lessons learned through time-consuming, expensive, and sometimes painful mistakes.

This easy seven-step process will help you start your business quickly while avoiding the many mistakes and challenges that you are bound to face if you go this journey alone. One of my goals in writing this book is to teach you the steps that I took so that you don't have to figure it all out by yourself. You don't need to reinvent the wheel. You get to benefit from all the energy, hours, and money I spent learning how to start and sustain a successful virtual assistant business.

This process will give you a huge head start towards realizing your dream of being a stay-at-home mom and a virtual assistant. You get to live life on your terms, making the money you want from home without compromising on the quality time that you desire to have with your family.

I mapped out these steps intentionally and purposefully to take you on a fast and easy path to accomplishing your dream.

To recap from the Introduction, the seven steps in the ALIGNED process are:

A – Assess Your Life

The first step is to get clear about what you want for yourself, for your family, and in your business. As you work through the worksheets that I designed, you will be able to assess where you are, what you want to accomplish, and your personal and family values.

L – Look Within to Find Your Assets

This is the most fun step. It's a journey of self-exploration. Through various tests and exercises that I've provided for you, you will discover who you are, your gifts, core values, skills, talents, strengths and weaknesses, love language, personality, spiritual gifts, and temperament. . This knowledge will help you be crystal clear about what services to offer your clients. It will also empower you to negotiate your fees with confidence.

I – Ingest and Integrate

Once you complete your "Assessment" and the "Look Inside Yourself" exercises, you'll do a detailed review of all your results and compile them in a single document. Ingest, relish, and appreciate the gifts, strengths, skills, and talents that you've been generously endowed with.

Next, you will integrate your self-discovery results with your goals. In this step, you may need to make some adjustments to your initial "Assess Your Life" results to align them with your core values.

G – Go! Get Your Business Started

Now that you know what you want and that you are equipped to accomplish your goals, this is where I charge you to "Go! Get Your Business Started!" It's time to get to serious work. This is where the rubber meets the road.

This part of the ALIGNED process details the steps required to start your virtual assistant business. It includes: skills, qualifications, and equipment that you need; different types of business structures for tax purposes; how to receive payments from clients; how to identify your ideal client and where to find them; how to bid for jobs; how to market your services; how to work with your first clients; how to grow and expand your business; and much more.

N – Nurture What You Create

This fifth step of the ALIGNED process, where you will learn various strategies to help you nurture and sustain the business you create. You will discover how to live out your core values in your business, how to serve your clients purposefully, how to build trust and nurture client relationships, and how to ask for referrals and testimonials.

E – Embrace and Enjoy

The sixth step is an essential one. You will learn how to embrace and enjoy your new life as a stay-at-home mom and business owner. I will teach you how to eliminate stress, overwhelm, and burnout. You will learn tips on how to manage and balance time between your business and your family. You will get tips on how to set clear boundaries and communicate them effectively.

D – Dream and Grow

This is the final step. Here you will learn about opportunities available for growing and expanding your business and yourself. You will discover some paths available for virtual assistants who want to maximize their gifts to fulfill their life's purpose.

You will learn that living in alignment with who you are as a powerful, nurturing, creative, life-giving woman means choosing to perpetually grow, expand, create, and give life to new dreams and ventures.

You will also learn how to replicate the ALIGNED process for every new dream you want to realize.

In the coming chapters, I will discuss each of these steps in a lot more detail. Now, let's jump to the first step: Assess Your Life.

CHAPTER 5
A – ASSESS YOUR LIFE

"Anyone can plot a course with a map or compass;
but without a sense of who you are,
you will never know if you're already home."
—*Shannon L. Alder*

This is the first and most important step in the ALIGNED process. This is where you assess where you are and what you want for yourself, your family, and your business.

Being clear about where we are, what we want, where we want to go, and how to get there is a fundamental step in realizing our dreams or accomplishing our goals.

This step requires that you spend some quiet time alone to really connect with yourself deeply so that you can pull from your soul the desires of your heart. This may be a difficult exercise, as oftentimes we mothers tend to focus on everyone else's needs but not our own. As natural caregivers, we prioritize caring for our spouses, kids, parents, friends, and siblings before we take care of ourselves. So I understand that this may be challenging or even uncomfortable, but it is a very crucial step that should not be skipped.

When you begin this process, you may find that you are totally blank. You may discover that you are absolutely clueless about what you want for yourself. You may have to fight to overcome feelings of guilt, as this step may seem selfish. But let me reassure you that if you are patient with yourself and stick with this process, you will be able to connect with your inner self and identify your needs, your wants, your desires, and your dreams. There are no right or wrong answers—and don't worry, nothing is carved in stone. This is an initial assessment; you will get an opportunity to review it and make any adjustments to it in the "Ingest and Integrate" step in Chapter Seven.

So, let's get started…

ASSESSMENT EXERCISE

Step One: Set Up Your Retreat

1. Find a quiet place where you can enjoy one hour of uninterrupted time. (You may break this into two thirty-minute sessions if you are unable to set aside a complete hour.) This could be a room in your house, your front porch, a park, your backyard, your dining table, or any other space. The idea is to have sacred quiet time where you can be alone and without distractions or interruptions. Early morning is ideal, but if that's not practical, pick the kids' nap time or any other time that works for you.

2. Make your quiet space as comfortable as possible. You could use comfortable pillows, play soft relaxing or inspiring music that you love, or light aromatic candles. Whatever makes your space feel relaxed and comfortable is what you want to do.

3. Get a journal and a pen.

Step Two: Journal

1. When you are ready to spend uninterrupted time in your retreat space, get comfortable and begin this exercise by getting very quiet in your mind.

Put away all your thoughts and bring yourself into the present moment. I personally do this through prayer. I invite God's presence and ask Him to bring to the surface the desires that He placed inside of me when He created me, the thoughts that He has about me, and His plans for my life. After you do this, or whatever process works for you personally, to calm your mind, move to the next step.

* * * * *

Answer the following questions *honestly***. Capture the thoughts and ideas that come to you in your journal. Allow these thoughts to flow freely as you write. There are no right or wrong answers—honesty is the perfect answer.**

Personal Assessment:

i.   What makes me really happy? What puts a smile on my face?

ii.   What makes me feel like everything in life is perfect or what would I want to have/exist for me to feel like life is perfect?

iii.   What makes me really sad?

iv.   What makes me angry?

v. If I had the power to change one thing in my life, what would it be?

vi. What's my greatest regret?

vii. If I was single and had no children or any other responsibilities or commitments (including a job, a family, or friends), what would I do with my time, energy, and resources?

viii. If I had all the money in the world, how would I spend it?

ix. What am I most proud of in my life?

x. What am I most grateful for in my life?

xi. If I could teach my kid(s) one thing, what would it be?

xii. What's one thing that I would like to accomplish in the next year?

xiii. What's one thing that I would like to accomplish in the next five years?

xiv. What's one thing that I would like to accomplish in the next ten years?

. . . . . .

Answer the following questions regarding your family. Capture the thoughts and ideas that come to you in your journal. Allow these thoughts to flow freely as you write. Remember, there are no right or wrong answers—honesty is the perfect answer.

<u>Family Assessment:</u>

    i.   What kind of family do I want?

    ii.   What values do I want my family to stand for?

    iii.   What kind of home environment do I want to create for my family?

    iv.   How do I want us to relate to one another as a family?

    v.   What kind of relationship do I want with my spouse (if applicable)?

    vi.   What kind of relationship do I want with my kids?

    vii.   What activities do I want my family to be involved in?

viii. How do I want to invest in my relationship with my spouse (if applicable)?

ix. How do I want to invest in my relationship with my kids?

x. How would I want my family to give back to our community?

· · · · ·

Answer the following questions regarding your business and money goals. Capture the thoughts and ideas that come to you in your journal. Allow these thoughts to flow freely as you write. Remember, there are no right or wrong answers—honesty is the perfect answer.

Business Assessment:

i. What kind of business owner do I want to become?

ii. How much money would I want my business to generate monthly?

iii. Where would I like to see my business in one year?

iv. Where would I like to see my business in two years?

v. Where would I like to see my business in five years?

vi. Where would I like to see my business in ten years?

vii. What environment or atmosphere do I want to create for my business?

viii. What type of experience do I want to give my clients through my business?

ix. What values would I like my business to stand for?

x. What kind of relationships do I want to have with my clients?

xi. Beyond making money, what else would I like my business to accomplish?

xii. Apart from working on my business, what other business and non-business related opportunities or ventures do I want to explore?

Your answers to these questions reveal your purpose, priorities, values, and growth opportunities, and your personal, family, and income or business goals.

After you complete this exercise, you will have a well of information, some that you may have been aware of and some that you had never really thought about. What you uncover will help you find clarity about where you are right now, what you want, and what you hope to accomplish in your personal life, in your family life, and in your business.

When coaching my clients, I go deeper. Together, we review the answers to these questions and classify the answers under the following categories: purpose or calling, priorities, growth opportunities, core values, and goals. We also work together to set up one-year, five-year, and ten-year goals that honor their immediate pressing needs and their values.

You can do this on your own as well, and I will show you how to in Chapter Seven, where we'll take a deep dive into step number three of the ALIGNED process: Ingest and Integrate. Before we do that, let's move on to another type of self-discovery in Chapter Six, where you'll excavate the gems that are buried within you.

CHAPTER 6
L – LOOK WITHIN TO FIND YOUR ASSETS

"There is no greater journey than the one you must take to discover all the mysteries that lie within."
—Michelle Sandlin

In my opinion, this is the most fun step in the ALIGNED process. You will embark on a journey of self-exploration to uncover the assets that are buried inside you.

You will need to set time aside to take various tests and to complete a worksheet to help you discover and list your skills, talents, strengths, and weaknesses; your love language, personality, spiritual gifts, temperament, and significant life experiences. But first, let's start by defining these terms.

DEFINITIONS

Skills: There are two types of skills: hard skills and soft skills. Hard skills are abilities you learn formally or informally. Skills that enable you to perform tasks or conduct activities. These include any hard skills you acquire in the process of earning degrees, diplomas, certificates, and any other courses that you complete through formal education and training. Hard skills may also be learned informally through observation. For example, although one may take a course on baking, one may also learn how to bake informally by watching someone else doing it. The same goes for skills like painting, chess, dancing, etc. One could learn these skills formally in a class or informally by observation and practice. Whatever the case, hard skills are learned abilities that you pick up over time.

According to Google, soft skills are "personal attributes that enable someone to interact effectively and harmoniously with other people." Examples of soft skills are: proactivity, pleasantness, problem solving, listening, leadership, innovation, team playing, communication, resourcefulness, etc. In other words, soft skills tend to be abilities that you have developed less intentionally than hard skills.

Talents: These are any special abilities that you were born with. According to CambridgeDictionary.com, a talent is "a special natural ability to do something well."

Singing, communication, sports, organization, playing instruments, and humor are examples of talents.

Work Experience: This is any result or outcome one has obtained as a result of working at a job or occupation, including volunteering and internships, for a period of time. Your work experience results from the continual application of your skills while performing tasks in such environments.

Significant Life Experiences: In relation to assets, these are events that have had a huge impact in your life. Major accomplishments or awards, meeting very influential people in society, traumatic events such as abuse or divorce, near-death experiences, car accidents, and chronic illnesses are examples of significant life experiences that may have had a tremendous impact on your life. Whether positive or negative, they have the potential to propel you or position you to walk toward your destiny. They often give strong clues about who and how we are supposed to serve.

Knowledge: According to Wikipedia, "knowledge is a familiarity, awareness, or understanding of someone or something, such as facts, information, descriptions, or skills, which is acquired through experience or education by perceiving, discovering, or learning. 'Knowledge' can refer to a theoretical or practical understanding of a subject."

In other words, knowledge is any information that you have about any subject matter that you acquired through experience, observation, or education. The difference between knowledge and skill is that skill is the application of knowledge.

Strengths and Weaknesses: According to the English Oxford Living Dictionary, strength is "a good or beneficial quality or attribute of a person or thing." Strengths and talents can be confusing to distinguish. According to GallupStrengthCenter.com, you build your strengths by refining your talents using your skills and knowledge.

Weaknesses are the opposite of strengths. These are areas that we are not good at. They could be things that we are not talented at or have no skill in. Weaknesses can be improved through intentional effort. You can decide to work on your weaknesses by taking the time to study a particular thing with the goal of improving at it.

My personal belief is, rather than focus on improving what you're not good at, refine what you *are* good at. It's just easier and more fulfilling to honor the talents, skills, and abilities that we already have, rather than focusing on what we don't have.

Love Language: Based on Gary Chapman's book, *The Five Love Languages*, your love language is the way that you express or experience love.

Personality: According to the American Psychological Association, "personality refers to individual differences in characteristic patterns of thinking, feeling and behaving." In other words, it is the sum total of what makes you unique, unusual, interesting, or distinct—your emotional qualities, ways of behaving, and belief systems or mindset. It's what makes you uniquely you!

Temperament: "Your temperament is the way you tend to behave or the types of emotions you tend to exhibit," according to YourDictionary.com. It is also your disposition.

SELF-EXPLORATION EXERCISE

Part One

Now that we know what all the terms mean, the next step is to uncover what assets we have in each category.

Write the answers to the following questions in your journal. These questions are designed to help you uncover your assets.

Hard and Soft Skills:

1. List all your formal educational training until now. Include the name of the institution,

program or course, and the main skills that you learned.

- For example:
- Institution: Career & Business Institute.
- Program: Diploma in Accounting.
- Skills: Cost accounting, financial reporting, and tax preparation.

2. List all your soft skills. Enlist the help of your family, friends, or co-workers if you need to.

Talents:

3. What do you think you are naturally good at?

4. What do people tell you that you're "a natural" at, or that you are good at?

5. What activities brought you the most joy and fun when you were a child?

6. What activities do you get so engrossed in that you lose track of time?

Work Experience

7. List your work experience to date. Include employment, self-employment, internships, and volunteer positions.

Life Experiences

8. List your greatest accomplishments so far—the things that you are most proud of or that have brought you the greatest joy and sense of fulfillment.

9. List any life-changing events, including painful or traumatic ones, that you've experienced.

Knowledge:

10. List the subjects or topics on which you have more significant knowledge or information than the average person.

Part Two

The second part of your self-exploration journey involves taking various tests to help you identify your personality, temperament, love languages, and strengths and weaknesses.

Carve out some time to take the following free online tests, and answer the questions as honestly as you can. The results from these tests are helpful in giving you valuable insight on who you are as a person. You may record the results in your journal or use blank worksheet from my website. You can download it here: www.stayathomemomsmakingmoney.com/book-worksheets

Love Languages Test:
www.5lovelanguages.com/profile

Visit this website and click on the "Learn Your Love Language" button to take your test. This test will help you discover your primary and secondary love languages. Your primary love language expresses how you naturally give and receive love. Knowing how you naturally give and receive love will help you serve your clients more effectively. For instance, if you express love by giving gifts, then having a "client appreciation" budget for client gifts would be a good idea.

If words of affirmation are how you naturally prefer to receive love, then you will benefit from seeking client feedback regularly so that you can feel encouraged, motivated loved by your clients. You may want to consider seeking client feedback every month.

As your relationship with your clients develops, you may consider asking them for their love languages. This will help you express love to them effectively. We all want to be seen and loved so I can guarantee you that your clients will be pleased by your efforts. They will shower you with praise and positive feedback when you speak their love language regularly.

Myers-Briggs Personality Test:
www.16personalities.com/free-personality-test

If you've never taken the Myers–Briggs Type Indicator˚ (MBTI˚) personality test, then you are in for a treat. This test identifies your personality type based on scientific research. Many of the people who I interact with seem to agree that the results of this personality test are reliable.

The test was developed to help us understand our personalities and those of others in our environments. It is based on the psychological personality-type research of Carl Jung.

The Myers–Briggs website states, "The best reason to choose the MBTI instrument to discover your personality type is that hundreds of studies over the past forty years have proven the instrument to be both valid and reliable."

Once you discover your personality type, take the time to read the full details provided to get a deeper understanding of your personality. Record your personality type and your impressions about it in your journal. Freely write down all your thoughts and feelings as they come to mind.

Open Four Temperaments Scales:
http://personality-testing.info/tests/O4TS

This is another fun test for information and educational purposes. It tests how we tend to behave or respond emotionally as we interact with people and our environments. This test helps you be aware of another facet of your personality: your temperament.

Strengths and Weaknesses Test:
http://richardstep.com/richardstep-strengths-weaknesses-aptitude-test

This is another great test. Relax and answer the questions as honestly as you can. I like this test because it uncovers so many qualities that we really never think of as strengths, or which we never had the language for.

Now that you've completed all the work in this chapter, get your journal and read back over your discoveries. I hope that you are in awe of who you are! That's the reason why I wanted you to do this self-exploration, so that you can be more aware of who you are, and what you have been endowed with by God. Now you can walk in confidence and authority, knowing that you have much to offer our world.

I encourage you to embrace these results and begin to walk in the fullness of this reality. Begin to exercise your gifts, talents, and strengths within your family, in your community, at work, or at church. Pay attention to the opportunities that present themselves. God will begin to lead you toward the exact plans and purposes that He has for you as you begin to live in the fullness of who you are and what you've been given generously.

When working with a coaching client, we create a master document with all her assets (the answers to all the questions and the test results) summarized in one place for easy reference. Do the same in your journal or you use worksheet on the resource page of my website at: www.stayathomemomsmakingmoney.com/book-worksheets. We also explore the uniqueness of her personality, temperament, strengths, weaknesses, knowledge, skills, talents, love languages, and significant life experiences and how they could be connected to her life's purpose. We set specific goals and strategies to help her walk in her identity and the gifts that she has been given.

You can download all the exercises in this chapter on my website at: www.stayathomemomsmakingmoney.com/book-worksheets.

If you would like to explore one-on-one coaching with me, you may schedule time on my calendar by visiting my website at: www.stayathomemomsmakingmoney.com/explore

Now that you have all this awesome information about yourself, you may be wondering what to do with all of it. In the next chapter, I will help you ingest, digest, and integrate it so that you can set goals and create a virtual assistant business that reflects who you are.

CHAPTER 7
I – INGEST AND INTEGRATE

> *"Vision without action is merely a dream.*
> *Action without vision just passes time.*
> *Vision with action can change the world."*
> —Joel A. Barker

So, what you do you think of your discoveries? Are you still amazed at who you are and the many marvelous assets that are inside of you? It takes time to integrate your assets, especially if you've never done any kind of self-exploration work before.

The first step is to receive and accept this information with gratitude. Then choose to be the person you were created to be. It's almost as if you have been introduced to parts of you that you were not acquainted with: Over the next days, weeks, and even months, take time to review your assets, do additional research to get a greater understanding of your temperament, MBTI° personality type, love languages, talents, and all your other assets. And as you do, maintain a posture of embracing and accepting who you are and how you are uniquely designed and divinely equipped.

Next, pull out the answers to the Assess Your Life exercises you did in Chapter Five. Review your answers in light of your newly discovered assets. Some of your answers may change. If they do, that's great! And if they don't, that's okay too. The idea here is to align what you want for yourself, your family, and your business with who you are and the assets that you have. You want to be working with integrity right from the start so that you have a solid foundation for your business.

Hopefully by now you realize that your assets are for the purpose of serving others and making a difference in your world. Knowing who you are and what you have helps you understand the value you bring to the table in every interaction that you have, whether it's with family, friends, co-workers, clients, or your community. This knowledge will help you stay in your lane rather than striving to be someone you were not created to be. You will be able to confidently work with clients, performing work that you have the greatest potential to excel in because you have your arsenal of assets.

As I promised in Chapter Five, I will help you integrate the information you collected in the Assessment worksheets. We will put all your answers into various categories, then transfer this information into a master document for easy access and reference. The categories that we'll use are: priority, purpose/calling, growth opportunity, core value, business core values, business persona, business idea, ministry opportunity, client-relationship type, or goal (personal or business). You may find that some of the answers fit in multiple categories. For instance, a ministry opportunity or your purpose could also be a business idea. The idea is to assimilate the results, then put them in a user-friendly format.

Before we go any further, let's define the categories so that you can easily identify where each answer belongs.

Priority: This is an activity, a fact, or a matter that is of high importance. For the purposes of this exercise, a priority item is anything that requires your immediate attention. **Purpose or Calling:** According to Merriam-Webster's, a calling is "a strong inner impulse toward a particular course of action," especially "when accompanied by conviction of divine influence." Purpose is the reason for which you exist or were created.

Growth Opportunities: These are potential areas in your life where there's a need to explore healing or emotional growth.

Core Values: These are your fundamental beliefs. A core value is what you stand for in life. It is very important to you and is usually very instrumental in guiding your decisions. Examples of core values are strong family relationships, healthy living, pursuit of higher education, travel, faith, personal growth and development, etc.

Business Core Values: These represent what your business stands for as an entity. Examples of a company's core values are innovation, creativity, integrity, customer satisfaction, excellence, etc.

Business Persona: This is the aspect of your character that you present to, or is perceived by, your clients when you are doing business.

Business Idea: A business idea is an opportunity to serve others by providing a solution to a problem in exchange for money. There are as many business ideas as there are problems in this world. Starting a virtual assistant business is a perfect example.

Ministry Opportunity: This is an opportunity commonly found within the Christian faith, where in following the example of Jesus Christ, you willingly choose to serve others by offering help, meeting a need, or providing relief or solutions, usually by employing or offering your time, energy, skills, gifts, knowledge, or financial resources. These could also be volunteer opportunities to give back to your community.

Client Relationship Type: This refers to the type of relationship you want to have with your clients. Examples could be: mutual respect, trust, care, or honesty.

Goals (Personal or Business): These are specified outcomes that you expect to accomplish in the future by making a commitment and taking defined steps to help you achieve your desired results.

Now it's time to review your answers in your Personal, Family, and Business Assessment exercises.

Personal Assessment Results:

Your answers to questions i and vii may have clues to your **Purpose or Calling.**

The answer to question ii indicates your current **Priorities.**

The answers to question iii, iv, v, and vi reveal **Growth and Ministry Opportunities.**

The answers to questions vii, viii, ix, x, and xi give you clarity about your **Core Values.**

Answers to question xii, xiii and xiv are your **One-, Five-, and Ten-year Goals.**

Family Assessment Results:

All the answers in the Family Assessment worksheet reveal your **Family Core Values.**

Business Assessment Results:

The answer to question i is your **Business Persona.**

The answers to questions ii to vi are your **Business Goals.**

The answers to questions vii to ix are ideas for your **Business Core Values.**

The answer to question x is the **Nature of Your Client Relationships.**

Answers to questions xi and xii are potential **Business and Community Service Ideas or Ministry Opportunities** that you could explore.

Be sure to complete the exercises in Chapters Five and Six before you start your business. Expect to experience "Aha!" moments as you discover your assets and true desires for yourself, your family, and your business. Also, keep the answers for the Hard and Soft Skills exercise in Chapter Six handy—you will need them for the next chapter, where you will get to determine whether starting a virtual assistant business is a viable option for you.

I hope you can see how this deep preliminary work sets a solid foundation on which to lay your business.

I didn't do this work before I started my business. I didn't know to. At that time, I focused on bidding for jobs or sought out clients solely based on my skills and abilities. If I had confidence that I could solve a prospective client's problem, I engaged them in a sales conversation and oftentimes they signed up to work with me.

Had I known about and done this initial work before I started my business, I would have had a much easier experience. I would have saved myself a lot of stress when making decisions, and I would have avoided doing things that I later regretted because I didn't have a clear understanding of my values or what I truly desired for myself and family.

Here's an example of one of my experiences to help you see my point: After two years of working with one particular client, I had to have a very difficult conversation with them. I had to let them go. We had a great relationship, and I did amazing work for my client. I learned a lot from them and the model of their business, for which I was very grateful. My responsibilities had also grown, and I was making more money than I did when I first started working with them. Everything seemed perfectly fine except for the fact that my conscience was not at peace. Although I had the right skills and performed great work for my client, the service he provided his clients went completely against my ethical code. As much as I tried to ignore the discomfort I felt inside, I could not silence the quiet voice—God's voice—inside of me that constantly reminded me that I was investing my time and energy serving a mission that I not only disagreed with, but that was completely contrary to my beliefs. It was against one of my core values.

Had I been clear about my core values and what I stood for *before* I started reaching out to clients and marketing my services, I may never have served this client in the first place. The good thing though was that my client was very understanding. He respected me for taking a stand for what I believed in, especially because I was willing to lose money to honor my convictions.

In another scenario, also two years into my business, one of my clients changed her company from online to a brick-and-mortar business. She loved me so much and was willing to pay me more to continue working with her at her new business location. That would have required me to relocate in order to live closer to her offices. However, because I too was self-employed, moving to work at her new location would have meant that I would no longer be a virtual assistant, since I would not be working remotely anymore. She wanted to hire me as an employee, which also would have meant that I would have had to forego my other clients and dedicate all my time to her on a regular nine-to-five schedule. In other words, I would no longer be a business owner. I rejected her offer, as good and as promising as it was, because it was not in alignment with my needs. The reason I started my virtual assistant business was because I wanted to have the freedom and flexibility to spend more time with my family as a stay-at-home mom.

I hope you can see why the first three steps of the ALIGNED process are critical pieces in laying a strong foundation for your business and life. You will make very many decisions in your business, but having completed this work, you will be able to position yourself to easily identify the right opportunities, choices, and decisions that align with your values and goals.

With that, we conclude Part One of this book. In Part Two, we will cover the next four steps in the ALIGNED process. We will first learn everything you need to start your business: the equipment you need; where to find clients; how to market your services; how to bid for jobs; how to avoid stress and burnout; how to nurture your business for long-term sustainability; how to recognize opportunities for growth; and much more.

PART II

CHAPTER 8
G — GO! GET YOUR BUSINESS STARTED

> *"The secret to getting ahead is getting started."*
> *—Mark Twain*

With all the preliminary work out of the way, it's time to get to the heart and soul of why I wrote this book. We're going to cover a lot of material, so please bear with me. I want to make sure that you have all the information I have so that you can start your business with the confidence and courage you need.

In this chapter, we cover the fourth step in the ALIGNED process. I will break down this step into short sub-chapters or sections so that you can tackle it bit by bit. But before we get started, I want to share with you some background information, statistics, and definitions. Did you know that small- and medium-sized businesses make up more than 70 percent of the businesses in the country? These are the mom-and-pop stores in your neighborhood, the local coffee shops, the farmer's market booths, the florists, the hair salons, the barber shops, the local daycare centers, etc. Although small, they have a huge impact on the economy.

What's surprising is that according to the Small Business Administration, only 50 percent of these businesses will survive within the next five years. The other 50 percent will close up shop, shut down, or file for bankruptcy within two years. There are many factors that contribute to the short life span of business start-ups.

From my experience working with many start-up businesses as clients, I would say a common reason why businesses fail is that although most business owners have great ideas and passion for their businesses, many lack the financial resources, skills, knowledge, tools, and patience to sustain their businesses for the long term. Passion and great ideas are important, but relevant knowledge or training in the business and industry that you are getting into are critical for success.

Succeeding in business is like raising children. As you discovered in the work that you did in the last three chapters, everyone—including children—is unique in their physique, strengths, weaknesses, personalities, gifts, talents, and temperament. This calls for unique parenting strategies for every child. The same applies to business. Every successful business adopts its own unique strategies in light of its strengths, weaknesses, threats, and opportunities.

A virtual assistant business is no different. It functions differently from a brick-and-mortar business. The business model of a typical brick-and-mortar business will be different from a virtual assistant business or any other online business. My point is that you can't apply just any business strategy and hope that everything will work out. Knowledge is your best friend.

(Please note: I will use virtual assistance or virtual assistant in an abbreviated form—VA—for most of the remaining part of the book to make reading easy.)

WHO IS A VA?

A VA is a self-employed contractor, usually a sole proprietor, who is hired to provide administrative support services from a remote location (virtually). A VA mainly works from the comfort of her home. However, some VAs choose to work from a coffee shop, a library, or a leased office. I've always preferred to work from home so that I could be with my babies when they were little. It's still my preference, even though my kids are now in seventh and fifth grade.

By definition, a VA assists or supports her clients. Depending on her skillset, she usually performs a variety of administrative support tasks such as:

- Email and phone customer or client support
- Email inbox management and filtering
- Prospects, leads, and customer follow-up
- Organizing meetings and presentations
- Data entry and management
- Research
- Basic bookkeeping and billing
- Travel planning and management
- E-calendar management
- Basic audio and video transcriptions
- Social media support
- Email marketing support
- Client Relationship Management software and shopping-cart support
- Personal errands such as gift and air-ticket shopping, hotel reservations, etc.
- Report preparation and presentation
- Scheduling online conferences, webinars, and teleseminars
- Blog and website updates, posts, comments, and general maintenance
- Setting up blog posts, e-newsletters, and e-zines
- Light graphic design (flyers, postcards, and handout creation)
- And more.

Now, review your answers for the "Hard and Soft Skills" exercise. If you can perform 50 percent or more of the tasks above, then starting a virtual assistant business is a viable option for you. If you can perform 25 to 50 percent of these tasks and you are willing to learn more skills, then you qualify as well. The nature of a virtual assistant business is that you are constantly learning, and the clients do not expect you to know everything. However, if you are proactive and willing to learn, your will be a valuable asset to your clients.

Other qualities that you must have as a virtual assistant are reliability, attentiveness to details, problem-solving abilities, a willingness to learn, excellent communication skills, and a get-tasks-done attitude.

If you have these qualities along with the skills above, you have passed with flying colors. You are capable of starting a successful virtual assistant business. If you have at least four of the six must-have qualities I listed above and are willing to work on the remaining two you qualify as well. A willingness to learn comes with the territory, so don't disqualify yourself even if you don't meet all the qualifications. As long as you're willing to acquire those skills, then you make the grade. As a person who offers these services and also hires virtual assistants, I would say that reliability is the most valuable characteristic that you can offer your clients. They want to know that they can count on you to complete the tasks assigned to you per agreed-upon deadlines.

I've heard people refer to virtual assistants as secretaries, but as you can see the tasks they perform are not limited to secretarial duties. A VA is hired to relieve the business owner of the workload that keeps her stuck in the day-to-day operations of her business, hindering her from focusing on revenue generating and business-growth activities that only she can perform. This is the primary role of the VA.

There are many other reasons why business owners need VAs, but here are just a few:

- A VA increases the human capacity of the business, enabling it to be more productive and profitable. Once a business owner hires a VA, they delegate tasks to the VA so that their own time is freed up and they can focus on income-generating activities, which lead to growth and profitability. A lot more is achievable with two people working on the business instead of one.

- Hiring a VA enables the business owner to focus on their specialized trade or area of expertise (e.g. fitness training, coaching, treating patients, etc.) instead of getting distracted by tasks such as sending thank-you notes to customers, researching, and following up on payments. Although these tasks are necessary and important, spending time on them at the expense of serving clients well or marketing and growing the business is not the best use of the business owner's time.

- It is more affordable to hire a VA than a full-time employee. Contracting the services of a VA cuts down expenses such as payroll taxes, employment benefits, continuous training costs, office rental, and office equipment.

- Most business owners enjoy their freedom. When they hire a VA, they look for an expert so that they don't have to spend a significant amount of time training. They also don't want to have to constantly be monitoring the VA's productivity. They want to have peace of mind, knowing that all the tasks assigned to the VA will be taken care of meticulously, professionally, and within agreed upon deadlines.

- Many small business owners work from their homes as well, and most of them would rather not have their assistants report to work at their home offices. That way they can enjoy their freedom and privacy.

TYPES OF BUSINESS STRUCTURES

You will need to consider several types of business structures before starting your business: sole proprietorships, partnerships, corporations (C and S corporations), and LLCs (Limited Liability Companies).

Do your research and consider talking to a business attorney or tax consultant so that you can make an informed decision. Different states and countries have different tax laws, so you want to make sure that you make the right decision for your business.

Out of ignorance, I skipped this step when I started my business and paid a hefty price for it. I did not consult a tax accountant before I chose my business structure, and two years down the road when I hired a tax consultant, he advised me that I had picked the wrong structure for the nature and goals of my business.

He filed for an adjustment so that the tax treatment of my business was more favorable to me, but that did not prevent me from paying the high taxes, penalties, and interest that resulted from choosing the wrong structure. I could have avoided this expense had I set my business up correctly from the beginning. So please, do your homework and set up your business properly.

CHOOSING YOUR BUSINESS NAME

Do you have any idea what you want to name your business? I think this is such a fun part of the process. Remember when you were researching your baby's name? How fun and exciting was that?

In the first few chapters of the book, I talk about how starting my business was a kind of birthing. Your business is the new baby that you're about to deliver into this world. You will be surprised to know that some of the things you considered when naming your kids are similar to what you will factor in when choosing the name of your business.

Some of the things to consider when deciding the name of your company are:

1. Is it memorable?

2. Does it give a clue to the type of service or product you offer?

3. Is the domain name available online, and easy to spell?

4. Are there other businesses that use the same name?

5. Is it easy to pronounce?

6. Does it give a positive mental image?

7. Is it an acronym? (Avoid acronyms because most people will not automatically understand what your acronym stands for)

There are many other factors that you could consider. Do your research and settle on a name that feels right.

Equipment and Materials That You'll Need:

You will need the following:

- **A reliable computer.** This could be an Apple or PC laptop or desktop with the capacity to store your client files. A computer with 500 GB of storage or more is adequate.

  You should also have Microsoft Office installed in your PC. The programs that you will use most frequently are Word, Excel, and PowerPoint. Some of your clients may have you work on Publisher or Access, but those are not very common. If you use an Apple computer, install the Mac version or the Apple equivalent, iWork.

Purchase and install reliable antivirus software to protect your computer. Some of the features to pay attention to when shopping for your antivirus software are:

- Prevents identity theft by protecting the data of yourself and your clients, such as email addresses, usernames, and passwords

- Prevents file deletion and unwanted changes

- Prevents fraudulent activities by safeguarding your online transactions

- Alerts you when there is suspicious activity

- Prevents viruses, spyware, malware, and other unwanted invaders from infesting your computer or from using your computer to attack other computers

- And blocks attempts to download potentially harmful programs to your computer.

The antivirus software that I like best is Avast. Avira is also very good. AVG is another one that's popular.

- **Reliable Internet connection.** A stable Internet connection is an absolute must. If the computer is your engine, a stable Internet connection is your fuel. Without a reliable Internet, you can't get much work done. About 95 percent of the communication in a VA's world is done via the Internet via email, Skype, Zoom, Google Hangouts, Slack, and other messaging apps. You want to make sure that you are accessible to your clients.

- **Video camera and headset.** These are optional, as they are dependent on your clients' needs. Some clients will want to meet you via videoconferencing software (e.g., Zoom, Skype, or Google Hangouts). A video camera shouldn't be a big deal because most computers come with a webcam, and cell phones come with video cameras.

  When selecting a headset, pick a noise-cancelling headphone. You always want to present yourself as a professional during phone or video-conference meetings with your clients. You also want to be able to hear clearly. Noise-cancelling headphones eliminate background noise around you, such as children crying, traffic passing, or a vacuum cleaner running.

- **Phone.** This is a no-brainer, but you will need a phone to get started. If you have a cell phone, that will work perfectly. As your business grows, you may decide to get a separate business cell phone and/or landline. If your cell phone is not a smartphone, you should invest in one so that you can download easy-to-use apps, such as video- and audio-recording apps, calendar and time-management apps, phone and chat apps, filing apps, and social media apps. These will not only improve your efficiency, they will also help you keep up with the trends. Most entrepreneurs look for new, efficient, and cost-effective systems, so you want to have a smartphone that will help you keep up with your clients.

- **Multi-functional printer with scanning capabilities.** These types of printers with scanning capabilities are very affordable nowadays. Although digital storage is very popular, there are important documents that you will occasionally want to keep hard copies of. You want to have the ability to scan or copy such documents for filing.

This printer will also come in handy when you need to convert hard copies into electronic copies for emailing, faxing, or to store in the cloud.

Depending on your clients' needs, certain tasks may require special equipment or software. For instance, if you're doing bookkeeping, you will need to use accounting software. If you're a transcriptionist, you will need to use transcription software, a pedal, and headphones. If you duplicate CDs for your client, you may need a CD duplicator. If these are your areas of specialization, then you should invest in these, as they are your tools of trade. However, if these are new skills that you are learning as you work with your client, your client may be willing to invest in the equipment or software so that you can learn and perform the necessary tasks.

Once, a client purchased Camtasia, screen-recording and video-editing software, for me to use to create training videos. The same client purchased a CD duplicator because he wanted me to learn how to duplicate CDs to mail out to his club members.

- **Marketing Materials**

When getting started, you want to keep it simple. When we complicate things, we are unable to focus. We get distracted and end up doing nothing. So, keep marketing simple and basic. Since you're just getting started, you want to focus on getting one client at a time. You don't want to have too many clients all at once because you may not be able to serve them each well if you're overwhelmed. You want to give your first clients your best service because you want to develop long-term, successful relationships with them and also get referrals and good reviews or testimonials from them.

With that said, remember that as a solopreneur, your capacity is limited. Your family is also a priority, so you want to be able to balance your business and your family life.

As your business grows and your capacity to manage clients increases, you can then move on to more elaborate marketing strategies.

Business cards and flyers—you will need these when you get started. You can design and order simple business cards and flyers to distribute to potential clients. They don't have to be fancy if you are on a tight budget. You can email e-flyers to your contacts or potential clients, or you can get them printed at your local print shop or order them online. Vistaprint.com is a great site where you can design and order business cards, brochures, and flyers.

If you want to get your business card designed by a graphic designer, Fiverr.com is the place to find freelance designers at affordable rates. At less than thirty dollars (as of the time of writing this book), you can get your business cards designed in just a couple of days.

You may also set up a Facebook, LinkedIn, or other social media page to get word out about your business. You can pick just one platform to start with; you don't have to use all three. I would not recommend investing in a website until you settle into your business and are clear about the services that you will want to offer or specialize in. However, you will still be able to market effectively with your business cards, flyers, word of mouth, and social media, and through freelance and networking sites that I will teach you about in this book.

DEFINE YOUR IDEAL CLIENT

Before you start looking for clients, it is important to first define your ideal client so that you can laser focus your marketing efforts to speak to the right target market. You want be clear about who you are looking for and where to find them.

Having completed the deep self-exploration, you now know your assets: your skills, abilities, strengths, weaknesses, experience, talents, temperament, and personality. You are clear about what you bring to the table.

Being clear about your skillset will help you determine your target market, i.e., who needs your services. For example, if you worked as an administrative assistant in a nursing home, clients in the health care industry—such as physicians, wellness practitioners, and other health-related businesses—could be great target markets. If you have a bookkeeping background, you may target clients who need services that include billing, accounting and reporting, accounts payable and receivable management, accounts reconciliations, or payroll, depending on your specific skillset.

Any specialized skills that you have, in addition to your general administrative support skills, make you more marketable and a valuable resource to your clients' businesses.

Now it's time to create your ideal client's profile. How would you know if a potential client is a good match? A business owner whose life and business corresponds with your skills, values, life, and business in a way that's complementary is a great match. The following exercise will help you identify your ideal client so that you can get clear in your mind about the type of client you want to work with. The more detailed your ideal client profile, the easier it will be to figure out where to locate your potential client and how to market your services effectively. Use your imagination and creativity for this exercise and feel free to add more questions to flesh out your ideal client profile further.

- What is your client's name?
- How old is your client?
- Is she or he married or single?
- How many children does your client have?
- How old are the children?
- Where does your client live?
- Does she or he rent or own his or her home?
- What car does she or he drive?
- How many cars does she or he have?
- What's your client's level of education?
- What did she or he study in college?
- What kind of business does your client have?
- Is it a sole proprietorship, corporation, or partnership?
- How many businesses does your client have?
- How long has she or he been in business?
- What is your client's annual business revenue?
- Does she or he have any employees? If so, how many?
- Why did she or he start the business(es)?
- What does your client do for fun?
- What does she or he do after work?
- What are your client's hobbies?
- Where does she or he spend her vacation?

- How often does she or he go on vacation?
- What's her or his favorite meal?
- What's her or his favorite TV show or movie?
- What are your client's religious beliefs?
- What charities does she or he support, if any?
- What keeps her or him awake at night?
- What brings her or him the greatest joy?

Here's a sample ideal client profile:

Jim is forty-two years old. He is married to Alicia, who is a stay-at-home mom. They have two daughters, twelve and ten years old, and a son who is six years old. They own their home in Sugar Land, Houston. Altogether they own three cars: a Chevy Tahoe, a Ford Edge, and a BMW convertible.

Jim has a bachelor's degree in business with a major in marketing. He was employed for five years after college, then ventured off to start his first business, which he sold recently. He ran his first business for ten years. He incorporated his new business six months ago. He sells health supplements online. His business is growing very fast and he is quickly realizing that he needs to build a team to support the growth of his business. He currently is a solopreneur working by himself.

The annual gross revenue of his first business was $600,000. His goal for his first year of the new business is $300,000, with projected gross revenue of $1 million by the third year.

He attends business expos, trade shows, and workshops regularly. He is a member of various business networking groups in Houston and also online.

He enjoys spending time with his family after work. He plays basketball and golf with his friends. He vacations with his family at least once a year during the summer. They travel to exotic destinations around the world. They go to California for Thanksgiving and New York during Christmas to spend time with both sides of their family.

Jim's favorite meal is his wife's homemade beef tacos. He enjoys watching basketball, football, America's Got Talent, *and* Shark Tank.

He goes to church on Sunday with his family, where he volunteers as an usher. He financially supports his church as well as nonprofit organizations that fight against human trafficking.

He worries about providing for his family well and maintaining his financial success. He never wants his wife to worry about money or have to look for a job because of the lack of it. He believes that his primary responsibility is to provide for his family and he wants to do it well. This is the reason why he works as hard as he does to make sure that his businesses are successful.

His greatest desire is to be a good husband and father to his kids and to give back to the community. His greatest satisfaction and fulfillment comes from knowing that his family loves him.

Now that you have your ideal client profile, your next question is probably, "Where do I find clients?"

WHERE TO FIND YOUR CLIENTS

There are various ways to find your ideal client.

1. **Word of Mouth**

   Start getting the word out about the services that you will be offering. If you have a good relationship with your boss, share your idea of offering VA services part time. He may be willing to have you start working as a VA remotely, and he would essentially be your first client. He may even be a part-time entrepreneur in need of your services. Your boss may also have friends and relatives who are small business owners whom he could recommend your services to. You just never know what opportunities are out there until you get the word out.

   In addition to talking to your boss, reach out to your colleagues and previous employers. You could also reach out to vendors and third parties with whom you have good relationships. These could potentially be your clients, or they could refer you to people in their networks who could benefit from your services.

Reach out to your family and friends. People assume that only established business owners need VAs, but that is not true. There are many people who are incredibly busy professionals and who do not have time to manage their personal lives. You could solve this problem for them by offering to become their virtual assistant. You can help them run errands remotely, shop online for groceries, pay bills, manage their family calendars, shop for gifts, make travel arrangements, etc.

As you spread the word about your service, always focus on how you will solve their problem, because that's what they are looking for. Simply telling them what you do or what services you offer will not get them to offer you the opportunity. Once they have a clear understanding of how you can help them, they are more likely to refer potential clients to you. Also, don't wait for them to send you referrals—be proactive in asking for them. Because they know you and they already have a level of trust that is easy to build on, they are likely to put in a good word for you to potential clients.

2. **Freelancer Sites:**

As mentioned earlier, freelance sites are online platforms where business owners search for freelance service providers. These sites offer short-term work to start with the possibility of long-term work if you hit it off with your client. Most small business owners look for virtual assistants who will support them as they focus on growing their business. If you start off well with a client, you may be on your way to enjoying a long-term relationship with them. I currently have a client that I've worked with for over five years.

Most freelance sites charge freelancers or business owners a service fee, transaction fee, or both. The service fees range anywhere from five percent to twenty percent depending on the platform.

Here's a list of freelance sites that you can use to find clients looking for your skills and service as a virtual assistant.

- **Upwork** – www.upwork.com
  Upwork is an online platform that connects business owners with freelance professionals. The business owners and professionals are required to create accounts in order to

benefit from the service. Upwork offers a free membership account and various paid membership account options for the freelancer.

The platform has sophisticated features that can allow you to build a team-based VA business. This means that if you decided to hire other VAs to work for you, Upwork allows you to assign tasks to your team members within the platform.

It also enables you to track your time as well as your team's time when working on your client's tasks. The platform has built-in time-tracking software that takes screenshots of the user's computer screens while working on a client's tasks or project. Your client is then able to review your work, determine if you understand your assignment, and get a sense of how fast you work or type to deliver a project or task.

You can choose how to be paid. The options available are: check, PayPal, or direct deposit to your bank account.

- **Guru** – www.guru.com
  Guru.com is similar to Upwork. It's a site that connects business owners with skilled

freelancers. It uses an escrow payment system called SafePay. Clients pay for your services in advance, as soon as they hire you for a job or project. The funds are held in the SafePay escrow account until you complete the assignment to the client's satisfaction and then the funds are released to you.

The escrow account acts as protection for you and your client. You can work confidently, knowing that your funds will be released and made available on completing the assignment. The client, on the other hand, has peace of mind knowing that their funds are in safe custody and will only be released once the job is completed to their satisfaction.

- **Freelancer** – www.freelancer.com
  This is an outsourcing marketplace similar to Guru.com and Upwork. This site connects business owners to freelancers. The potential client posts a job, and then the freelancers bid. The client then selects the freelancer with the winning bid. Freelancer. com hosts millions of freelancers, which makes it highly competitive. It offers both a free and paid membership account option.

- **FlexJobs** - www.flexjobs.com
  FlexJobs is a paid online resource for remote or telecommuting freelance opportunities. It offers monthly, quarterly, and annual subscription plans to choose from. FlexJobs does rigorous research to ensure that only high-quality job opportunities are posted on their website. In addition to the remote job posts, they provide resources to support you while you search for clients.

In conclusion, please note that the platforms I've highlighted above are not the only places where you can find clients online. However, these are the most popular platforms as of the time of writing this book.

3. **VA Companies:**

- **Zirtual** - www.zirtual.com
  Zirtual offers full-time jobs to VAs who are college educated and reside in the US. They have a rigorous application process, as only two percent of applicants are hired.

- **Fancy Hands** - www.fancyhands.com
  Fancy Hands hires virtual assistants in the US to complete various administrative tasks. They have VA positions and

managerial positions to manage VAs on their team.

- **Virtual Office VA** - www.virtualofficeva.com Virtual Office VA hires US-based VAs. They specialize in real estate investors and provide their VAs with the necessary training to support their real estate investment clients. Some of the tasks you will be expected to perform are research, calling sellers, answering inbound phone calls, and running marketing campaigns.

4. Networking Groups

Joining networking groups both online and offline is an additional way to find potential clients. Some VAs subcontract their projects and tasks when they have more work than they can manage. Developing relationships with other VAs within these networking groups can be an amazing opportunity to get part-time projects and tasks. These groups provide a lot of support, advice, encouragement, information, referrals, and opportunities that you could greatly benefit from.

A great networking group to consider joining is VA Networking. VA Networking is a free social network that supports VAs. Their mission is to maintain a quality community that helps VAs earn wealth and respect. They offer different types of trainings, free resources, and client referrals to support and empower VAs. I highly recommend this network.

There are many Facebook VA networking groups that you could join. Some that you may want to consider joining are: <u>Virtual Assistant Empowerment Group</u>, <u>Virtual Assistant Savvies</u>, <u>Virtual Assistant Connections</u> (based in Australia). There are many others that you can research and join as well.

5. **Social Media Sites**

Promoting your business through Facebook, Pinterest, Twitter, Instagram, or any other social media site is a great way to get exposure for your business. I am not an expert in social media marketing, but I do know that there are very many free and paid resources that are available online. One social media expert I recommend is Sandi Krakowski. You can follow her on Facebook, take advantage of her resources, or buy her training programs. I like her courses because she focuses on small business owners. She is also relatable and inspiring.

To start off, simply let your friends and followers on these platforms know about your services and ask them to recommend or refer you to people in their networks who may be interested in hiring you. You could also take advantage of social media groups that you are currently in and do the same. Let them know about your new venture and ask them for referrals.

Once you have a few paying clients and a marketing budget, you can then invest in social media trainings and paid advertisements on these sites.

NAVIGATING FREELANCE SITES

In this section I want to focus on how to successfully navigate and find clients in freelance sites because they have their own unique process to follow.

How to Create Your Freelance Master Profile Template

Freelance online platforms are websites where business owners search for skilled freelancers or service providers. Business owners post their job or project requirements then qualified freelancers or service providers respond by placing their bid. The business owners then go through a short-listing and interview process to identify the right candidate.

I want us to focus on creating a freelance master profile template because most of the freelance platforms will require you to create a profile. This is where you showcase yourself. The goal is to present yourself as an expert virtual assistant so that your potential clients will want to hire you. Keep the work that you did in the "L – Look Inside to Find Your Assets" worksheets handy. You will need to refer to them multiple times as you create your profile.

Upwork.com is one of the freelance sites that I listed earlier in this chapter. I will use the Upwork profile requirements to help you create a master profile template in MS Word. Your template will store all the information you need for creating your profiles on different sites in one place. You will then copy and paste or tweak the relevant information for the various freelance sites as needed. Many of these freelance platforms require similar information.

Before you create your profile on any freelance site, make sure that you follow the instructions below and create your master profile template in MS Word or Pages. Some of the sites are very strict and will not approve your account if your profile is not detailed or is incomplete. It's important that your profile is impressive so that you are granted membership on the freelancer sites. For this reason, you want to create a profile that stands out.

Your Master Profile Template

1. Photo

Get a high-quality, professional head shot. A profile picture with you smiling and in a professional outfit will make a good first impression.

2. Profile Title

Create an attention-grabbing title for your freelance profile that is simple and to the point. A title is a short, descriptive benefit statement or headline. It should be less than ten words. It should speak directly to your ideal client. It should answer your ideal client's problem.

Almost all business owners who are looking for a VA want to hire one so that they can free up their time by delegating daily administrative tasks to the VA. They want to focus on their area of expertise, marketing, and growth activities.

By the time a business owner is looking for a VA in Upwork or any other freelance site, they are usually feeling stuck, frustrated, and desperate. They have tasks backlogged, unpaid bills, customer emails that have gone without replies for days or weeks, phone calls unanswered, voice mails unreturned, products undelivered, articles and blog posts still stuck in their brains unwritten, and social media accounts dead from inactivity. You get the idea?

So, they need your help. They want a reliable person to help them bring order to their business. They also want to have the peace of mind that comes from knowing that they have someone on their team that they can count on. They are banking on a skilled VA to handle the daily administrative and back-office tasks consistently and in a timely fashion so that they can focus on serving their customers or clients, implementing marketing strategies, getting new clients, and such activities that only they can perform.

Therefore, your title should speak directly to what these clients need. It should highlight the greatest benefits that you bring to the table.

For instance, if you want to focus on, say, business owners who use Infusionsoft as their CRM tool, your title should communicate the greatest benefit your client will receive from hiring you. Here's an example of an attention-grabbing title or headline for a VA who is an expert in Infusionsoft: **Never Waste an Extra Minute Trying to Figure Out Infusionsoft Again!**

Infusionsoft is one of the most popular and highly recommended CRM software programs. However, it's not an easy tool to learn. The learning curve is steep. Therefore, a VA who is skilled in Infusionsoft is one that would be highly sought after by business owners who use Infusionsoft. Such a VA will potentially save the business owner a lot of stress, time, and energy that they would have otherwise invested in learning the software, which is not the best use of their time. His time could be better spent in his area of expertise.

If you want to specialize in customer service and are targeting coaches, the benefit that your client will get should be clear. Here's an example of an attention-grabbing title for the VA who wants to specialize in being a customer service representative for business and life coaches: **Rockstar Client Concierge Who Makes You Look Like a Pro!**

Although I didn't mention business or life coaching in the title, "Client Concierge" is a term that many coaches use to refer to customer service representative. So this title will grab the attention of coaches.

3. **Overview**

This is where you will write a short commercial (advertisement) about yourself. It is a summary of the benefits your clients will receive from working with you. Include at least three compelling reasons why a potential client should hire you as their VA.

Some of the things you could highlight are: your expertise, the niche you specialize in, the systems and programs that you are competent in, your hard skills and relevant soft skills, your accomplishments, and anything else that would capture your potential client's interest. Refer to the work we did in the "L – Look Inside to Find Your Assets" worksheets to pull any additional information that is useful.

A testimonial from a former employer will also enhance your profile because that gives you credibility.

The overview is not your autobiography, so don't include any information that doesn't promote your services. The key ideas here are clarity and simplicity: The simpler and more concise your overview is, the more appealing it will be.

Use bullet points to make your overview easy to read. Flesh out your bullet points with one sentence to help explain or to give examples to back up each point.

As you write your overview, put the most important and relevant information first. Within the Upwork platform, only the first two or three sentences are visible at first glance. The client would need to click on "Read More" to read the rest of your overview, which they may or may not do. Therefore these three sentences are prime advertising real estate, so maximize your use of the space.

4. **Media File**

The media file section is another piece of advertising real estate to advertise your services. You can use photos, graphics, videos, or audio recordings. A picture is worth a thousand words, they say, but how about a video? Is it worth a million words? My point is: Take advantage of this section to upload relevant audio files, videos, photos, or graphics.

Many freelancers skip this section. Make sure you use this space so that you can stand out from the crowd.

5. **Introduction Video**

Create a short, clear, video thirty seconds to one minute long to introduce yourself. The video will give potential clients insight to who you are, your personality, and your unique qualities. It will give them an idea of what to expect while working with you. Let your awesome personality shine as you create your introduction video. Be upbeat, warm, pleasant, and passionate about the work you do.

Write a script using the template below. Practice it until you can record the video without reading the script. Use a high-quality video camera. (Most phone cameras take good videos, so this should not be a problem. At a later date, when you have made money in your business, you can invest in a professional videographer and update the video on your profile.) Pick a very quiet space with good natural lighting. Use a simple, clutter-free background to eliminate distractions—you want your potential client to focus on you, not your background. Upwork recommends that you position yourself off-center (rather than right in the middle of the screen). Make sure that you are visible from your waist up, including your hands, so that all your hand gestures can be captured. You may need to do several video takes to check lighting, the camera angle, how you are positioned in the video, the audibility of your voice, your demeanor and aura, and the overall quality of the video, then pick your best video.

Here's a script template you could use to create your video.

Introduction (5–10 seconds)

Who are you? What problem will you solve for your client? *How* will you solve their problem (using your services or area of expertise)? How long have you been offering your services? If you are just starting and don't have any experience as a virtual assistant, you may focus on your past work experience that is relevant to the services that you will provide.

Here are two examples to help illustrate how you may address the issue of lack of experience when you create your video.

An experienced customer service VA may say, *"I have been providing customer support services for the last three years."* While an inexperienced VA may say, *"I have three years of customer service experience."* Do you see the subtle difference? Both VAs have the same skill and experience. However, one has been a virtual assistant for three years while the second one is just starting out. She does not highlight her lack of VA experience, as this would place her at a disadvantage. I hope that makes sense. Always market yourself favorably.

Objective (10–20 seconds)

What clients do you work with? What is your target niche or market?

Professional Highlights (10–20 seconds)

What professional experience illustrates your expertise or credibility? (Give an example of a success story. You could read a testimonial from a client or from a previous employer.)

Conclusion (5–10 seconds)

What actions do you want your potential client to take after watching the video? (For example: "Send me a message to let me know when you would like to schedule a phone conversation to discuss your needs in detail." Then give specific instructions on where to send the message: an email address or phone number, or your contact information via the freelance site.)

Once you've created your video, you will need to upload it to YouTube, then follow the instructions in Upwork to upload the video to your profile.

6. **Skills**

For this section, Upwork provides a list of skills for you to select from. Select the skills that you are highly proficient in first, or those that match the needs of the clients that you want to work with. Once your profile account is completed and approved by Upwork, the system will match you with clients who are looking for your skills. Therefore, you should be sure to select all your relevant skills from the list.

Upwork also has some skill-based assessment tests. Take the time to complete them. The tests are optional except for a very simple one, which tests your basic knowledge of the Upwork platform. I recommend that you take a few additional tests. The more thorough and complete your profile is, the more likely it is the Upwork team will accept your application.

Upwork will allow you to retake the tests if you get a low score or if you want to improve your score. If you do retake a test, the site gives you the option to hide the results from the initial test.

7. **Portfolio**

The portfolio section is where you show the quality of your work. It complements the information you provided in the "Overview" and "Skills" sections. Display your best work so that potential clients can see your level of competence and expertise.

The exercises you did in Chapter Six and Chapter Seven come in handy for this section. However, if you completed all the exercises in these two chapters, you should know what services you will be offering. If any of them require specialized and not general administrative skills, this is the section where you would upload samples of your work. I will cover more details and list examples of specialized skills in Chapter Eleven.

But for now, here's an example, you could upload a few of your best articles if you want to specialize in blogging. If you specialize in customer service, you could upload a file of email responses that you've crafted to show your expertise in that area. If you've designed handouts for workshops, you could upload samples of your work as part of your portfolio.

Be sure to get permission from your previous clients (or employers) before you upload the work if you don't have proprietary rights. Stay clear of breaching any confidentiality & nondisclosure agreements that you may have signed.

A testimonial document is also a good addition in this section. You may ask your previous clients, employers, supervisors, or colleagues to write testimonials or recommendation letters that you could compile into one document and upload in this section of your profile. This will give you instant credibility.

8. Employment History

List any work history, including dates, that's relevant to the services that you want to provide and to the clients that you want to serve. Focus on what will set you apart from all the other VAs on the platform. For example, your potential client would be more interested in your previous administrative assistant experience than your retail or pet-sitting skills.

The duration and pattern of your previous work history gives clues about your level of loyalty and reliability. Long-term clients look for VAs who have had client relationships or jobs for at least two years.

9. Certification

Scan and upload your certificates. Always make sure the scanned documents are clear and legible. Your certifications show your training and knowledge in specific subjects or areas (e.g., Infusionsoft certification).

10. Education:

Most clients are interested in your experience more than your education. However, your education background can enhance your profile because it validates your credibility.

Your potential client will receive applications from many VAs. They may use education to shortlist the applicants. So, don't leave it to chance. List your educational credentials in chronological order, starting with your most recent degree, diploma, or certificate.

Important notes to remember:

- Your profile is *not* a proposal or cover letter that needs to be sent out again and again. You will create your profile only once when you sign up with Upwork or any other freelance site. Once your Upwork account is approved, you can make changes to it.

- Once you've created your detailed profile, you will not need to upload your resume—your profile will act as your resume.

- In addition to creating your profile, you will write proposals to bid for jobs as they are posted by potential clients on freelance platforms.

- In order to be successful as a virtual assistant, you will need to build relationships with your clients that will be based on trust. Be honest—do not lie about your skills, experience, or expertise. Do not present other people's work as your own. It will only hurt you in the long run.

- Update your profile regularly as your skills and experience increase. Get rid of outdated or irrelevant information that no longer meets your clients' needs. For additional resources on how to create your profile in Upwork, visit the Upwork website.

HOW TO BID FOR JOBS

After creating your profile on a few of the freelance sites, the next thing you will want to do is bid for jobs. There are two ways to bid: You may look through the sites to identify job posts that match your skills then submit your bid or respond to clients who reach out to you directly and invite you to submit your bid.

Here are my tips for writing winning bids that will grab your prospective client's attention:

1. **Pay attention to the client's requirements.**

   When bidding for a job, make sure you read and understand the client's needs before you write your proposal. Address each question or requirement that the client lists in the job post. This shows that you pay close attention to details—a valuable skill that many business owners are looking for in a VA.

   If you have questions or need clarification, send a message to the client before you submit your proposal. This shows the client that you are interested in the job and have paid close attention to the job requirements. Also, because of your interaction, the client is more likely to pay more attention to your proposal.

2. **Make sure your profile stands out.**

If the client is impressed by your proposal, the next thing they will review is your profile. Make sure that you followed the detailed steps I outlined in the "Create a Profile" section so that your profile stands out from the crowd.

3. **Draft a customized proposal or cover letter.**

Different freelance sites will use terms like "proposal" or "bid," letter," but these mean the same thing. Bidding for a job on a freelance site is like applying for a regular office job. When you apply for work, you submit a cover letter with your résumé. The same applies for the freelance websites. Your profile is the equivalent of your résumé, and your proposal or bid is the equivalent of your cover letter.

The proposal or bid is where you explain in detail why the client should hire you and not all the other VAs who submit their proposal. When writing your proposal, you need to be client focused and solution oriented. You need to understand the client's needs or problems based on the information provided in the job post, then explain how you will solve the problem and why you are the best candidate for the job.

Take your time when creating your proposal. You only have one chance to impress your client, so take full advantage of the opportunity to make a lasting first impression. Customize and personalize your proposal as much as possible so the client feels that you understand their need and that you are the best fit.

For example, a simple VA job post may look like this:

Looking For: Full-time VA

Native English speaker with excellent communication skills. Responsibilities include: Google Calendar management and syncing with TimeTrade and iCalendar.

Setting up appointments, managing my inbox, replying to customer service emails, and handling other administrative tasks as needed.

Must be available to work at least 4 hours a day within the hours of nine a.m. to five p.m. PST.

Happy bidding!

As you bid for the job, you should address every requirement listed in the job post, explain how you would solve the problems presented, and show why you are a credible candidate.

For instance, your proposal you could say:

Hello, [Client's Name],

Thank you for the opportunity to bid for this job.

My name is Asia Brown and I'm very excited for this opportunity. I would be very happy to relieve you of the tasks that you've listed in your post so that you can focus on other parts of your business.

*I am t*he right candidate for this job because I have the exact skills and experience needed:

- *Excellent communication skills: I speak and write native American English fluently.*
- *Calendar Management: I have experience in scheduling appointments and managing and syncing various calendars, including Google, iCalendar, Acuity, and TimeTrade.*
- *Email Management: I previously worked as a gatekeeper for my client by managing her inbox. I organized her emails by labeling them as Urgent, Important, and Low Priority. This helped her prioritize and manage her time effectively.*
- Customer Service: I also have five years of customer service experience. I will help you create canned responses for I'm available from nine a.m. to five p.m. PST.

I hope you will giv*e me the opportunity to be of service to you and your business.*

I look forward to hearing back from you.

Sincerely,

*Asia B*rown

In the example above, Asia was not just addressing the need, but also her willingness to go an extra mile—a quality that many business owners appreciate.

4. **Make your proposal stand out.**

Your potential client may receive hundreds of proposals. Therefore, you must make sure your proposal stands out. Here are some tips on how to do just that:

- Keep your cover letter or proposal brief and concise. Rather than writing five to ten long paragraphs, write a short but powerful proposal. It should only take up to three main paragraphs to do that. The client will not have time to read your proposal and the other hundred that are waiting to be read. So make yours short, precise, and to the point.

- Proofread your proposal for typos and grammar errors before you submit it. As a

VA, you will be required to communicate in writing frequently. Your potential client will pay attention to your writing skills as she reads your proposal.

- Research your client's business. Do your due diligence. Learn as much as you can about your potential client before you bid. They may have created a detailed profile within the freelance platform where you found the job posting. Visit their profile page to learn more about them and what they do. Read the feedback they got from other service providers who worked for them. You can also use Google to find their website to learn more about their business and visit their social media pages to know more about them and their business.

All the information that you gather from your research will help you craft and customize your proposal and will also come in handy during an interview—going this extra mile will impress your client. It shows that you are serious about the job and are interested in understanding more about their business and the services or products that they sell.

- Use your connect(s). This is specifically for the Upwork platform, which uses the "connects" system. Connects are tokens that you use to submit proposals. Each job post is assigned a specific number of connects. The assigned connects are the minimum number of connects required to submit a proposal. If you sign up as a free user in Upwork, you are given 60 free connects a month. Paid members get more connects per month.

  The number of connects you use to submit your proposal determines the placement of your proposal on your potential client's account. It's like buying prime advertising space. The more connects you use, the higher your proposal is placed and the greater its visibility.

Your valuable time and energy are like connects: You only have so many to put into each bid. Use more of these resources on bids that you are especially excited about to be sure that they will stand head and shoulders above the competition.

5. Price your services right.

Pricing your services right is something every VA struggles with at the beginning. Most newbies in the US start at fifteen to twenty-five dollars per hour as they get their feet wet. However, if you have a strong administrative support background or you are specializing in a specific skill (e.g. Infusionsoft), then you should start at a higher rate. Seasoned VAs charge between thirty and fifty dollars per hour, depending on their mix of services and skills.

Upwork gives you the option to bid per project or per hour. It is usually difficult for both the VA and the client to accurately estimate how long it will take to complete a project or a variety of tasks. Therefore, it is best to bid using an hourly rate in the freelance platforms.

You can use other pricing methods with clients that you acquire outside the freelance sites. For instance, you could bundle up your services in a package and charge your clients a flat monthly rate. Or you can bundle basic administrative tasks in one package—tasks that require more expertise in a separate package from those that require less, and so on. This pricing method increases freedom, as you will be charging for the value or results you bring to your client and not for your time.

Some virtual assistants charge a monthly retainer. They perform tasks up to a certain number of hours per month, and for anything over and above the monthly flat rate, they charge an hourly rate.

Most of the freelance sites require that you provide an hourly rate, and most of the clients that you get through these sites will have that expectation. However, you can use the service package or retainer method with clients who come to you through your other marketing efforts.

6. Be honest.

Do not exaggerate your experience or expertise when bidding. Do not say that you are available from eight a.m. to five p.m. when in reality you are available from nine a.m. to three p.m. It will only be a matter of time before these lies catch up with you. You and the client may end up very frustrated if you're not able to live up to your promises. The client will be dissatisfied with your services and may give you negative feedback.

Your business reputation matters. It is better to be honest about what you can and cannot do than to destroy your credibility by underperforming or under-delivering.

Your best source of new business is happy clients. Make every effort to ensure that your clients are happy. Being honest is a great place to start.

HOW TO PREPARE FOR INTERVIEWS

> *"It is better to be prepared for an opportunity and not have one than to have an opportunity and not be prepared."*
> —*Whitney M. Young, Jr.*

Congratulations! You have been invited for your first interview.

A potential client who is interested in a long-term virtual assistant will interview you to see if you are a good fit for her business. In most cases, the client will suggest available dates and times for your interview. Try as much as possible to avail yourself of the suggested times. The client will interview several candidates, so you want to be sure that you get your interview time scheduled as soon as possible.

How to present yourself during an interview.

Your client will likely interview by phone, Skype, Google Hangouts, or Zoom. The client will usually be the one who suggests the platform through which they will interview you. If your interview will be conducted via webcam, do the following to prepare:

- **Find the best spot in your home for the interview.** Choose a clean, neutral background. Avoid a busy background to minimize distractions.

- **Choose a quiet space for the interview.** Keep the kids busy and away from your designated interview room. You do not want to have kids screaming and running in the background during your interview. It is unprofessional.

- **Do not have your interview in a coffee shop.** It's impossible to control background noise and distractions in public places. Always remember that you want to give your client a good first impression.

- **Check your equipment.** Test your microphone and video before the interview. Adjust your webcam to make sure the client can see your face properly. It is best to invest in a high-quality headset that can cancel outside noise. Make sure that you have the software or application that the client will use for the interview already installed. If the client suggests software or a conference service that you are not familiar with, do some research on Google, download it if need be, and test it prior to your interview.

- **Choose what to wear.** Dress as though you are going for an in-person interview. Smart casual or formal is appropriate. Present yourself as the kind of professional your client would want to work with.

- **Groom yourself.** This may sound obvious, but sometimes people disregard the importance of basic grooming. Make sure you comb your hair, wash your face, and apply light makeup if necessary. Avoid looking as if you have just woken up or come from the gym. Treat your virtual interview just as you would an in-person office interview.

- **Review the job post** and your proposal prior to the interview so that the information is fresh in your mind. The client is likely to ask you questions about your proposal. If you plan to submit or refer any documents to the client, have them readily available during the interview.

- **Be on time.** Show up at least five minutes before your interview. Being late for an interview not only shows a lack of respect for your client's time, but also gives a terrible first impression. If the client doesn't show up within the first ten minutes, send them a message right away to notify them that you are waiting for them.

- **Confirm your appointment** at least a day or two prior to the interview. Sometimes clients forget, or there may be a conflict on their calendar that just occurred.

How to Conduct Yourself During the Interview:

- Greet the client.

- Keep your hands on or under the table so that they are not visible on the screen, especially if you tend to fidget.

- Breathe and stay calm. Take advantage of pauses during the interview to take deep breaths.

- Maintain eye contact. Look directly into the webcam and not at your computer screen. You will look awkward on their screen if you do not look directly into the webcam.

- Pay attention to the client's personality. Does he or she seem talkative, easy going, or casual? This will give you clues as to whether you can engage in casual talk with them to build rapport.

- Speak slowly and clearly so that you don't have to repeat yourself. This is especially true when you are using a microphone.

- Be pleasant. Smile.

- Promise only what you can deliver.

- Be honest.

- Thank your interviewer for his or her time.

An interview will usually take about thirty to forty-five minutes. After your interview, send your client an email reiterating your appreciation for their time and for considering you for the interview. Remind the client of what you can contribute to their business and emphasize how much you look forward to working with them.

Very few people do this final yet simple follow-up step. This step could literally be the reason you get hired, because it really makes you stand out. It makes your professionalism and interest in the position very evident.

I want to mention though that interviews will usually be scheduled and conducted by potential clients looking for virtual assistants through freelancer sites, classified ads, or by virtual assistant companies looking to fill open positions in their organizations. However, when you find potential clients through referrals from your friends, followers on social media sites, word of mouth, or your networking efforts, you are the one who will schedule and conduct interviews with them. During these interview, you will find out their needs and determine whether you are able to help them and whether you are a good fit.

Thank you for staying with me. I know we have covered a lot of material in this chapter. To wrap up, here's a quick recap of what you've learned:

- Who is a virtual assistant

- Types of business structures

- How to name your business

- Equipment and materials needed

- How to create your freelance master profile template

- Defining your ideal client

- Where to find clients

- How to bid for jobs

- How to prepare for interviews

CHAPTER 9
N – NURTURE WHAT YOU CREATE

> *"The master of the garden is the one who*
> *waters it, trims the branches, plants the seeds,*
> *and pulls the weeds."*
> —Vera Nazarian

After you've been working with your clients for some time, you may start wondering what you need to do to maintain long-term relationships with them or how to guarantee their satisfaction with your services. The answer to this question is consistency! If you keep showing up for your clients consistently, they will come to depend on you. A long-term relationship will form because they can count on you.

By its very nature, virtual assistance is part of the service industry. Being that it's in the character of what we do, we decided to take on a servant's heart at my business. We do all our work from a place of love. We prioritize our clients' needs. Unbeknownst to our clients, we often pray for them, the success of their businesses, and their families.

Bringing a heart of service into our business automatically makes us stand out from the crowd. Many people are in business primarily for money. There's nothing wrong with that. However, when you serve people wholeheartedly with humility and love, hearts are touched, and lives are changed. People tend to reciprocate with gratitude, appreciation, and love. And a beautiful relationship is formed, founded in mutual respect and love.

It's very fulfilling to be in a virtual environment where love, trust, respect, and gratitude consistently flow between you and your clients.

I didn't start my business with a clear understanding of what my core business values were. It took time for me determine what I wanted my business to represent and to stand for. Over time I identified four critical areas where I needed to show up consistently over the course of running my business. They form the acronym "RICE." I decided to make them these the core values for my business and recently taught them to my team because I wanted everything we did to be rooted in these four standards.

The core values represented by the acronym RICE, which we adopted in my business are:

- **R – Reliability:** Be consistently reliable. Reliability will help build trust with your clients. Your clients will want to work with you regularly because they know that they can count on you to deliver what you promise without fail.

  One of my clients, Marley, knew that she could depend on me to get work done. In a testimonial, she said:

  Karen is the Program Manager of two of my coaching programs. She has done an excellent job of making sure that my programs run smoothly and my students are happy. She is also responsible for executing my email promotional campaigns; ensuring that my websites and blogs are up-to-date; reporting various metrics; managing orders and tracking payments, just to list a few of her responsibilities. Karen is all-rounded, reliable, and trustworthy—you can count on her to get work done. She's plays an important role in my company and [I] highly recommend her services.

- **I – Integrity:** This is our second core value. Having integrity is important for our core values, our goals, and ourselves. Maintaining integrity has helped us remain steadfast in how we interact and conduct business with our clients and team members.

Your clients will get to know you and what you stand for as your relationship develops. A relationship built on respect will be forged if you are a person or business who esteems trust. Your clients will want to keep working with you because they will respect you.

Maria, my very first client, was able to see my personality, integrity, and work ethic within a short time of working together. She wrote:

I hired Karen in February 2009 as a virtual assistant. Back then, my company was just a fledgling start-up involved in publishing books marketed through the Web. Karen very efficiently handled every facet of administrative work that could be done virtually, since we didn't have an office at that time. She effectively handled all customer service inquiries via email or Skype. She is well loved by our customers, clients, JV partners, and affiliates because of her professional, knowledgeable, yet friendly way of handling business affairs.

I can't recommend her highly enough. She was my first-ever full-time virtual assistant, who later took on customer service management. Her work ethic and efficiency are of the highest standards. —Maria Veloso, CEO, Think-Outside-the-Book Publishing, LLC

- **C – Care:** Our third core value is Care. We truly care about our clients and the success of their businesses. You can't fake caring. Your clients will know if you genuinely care about them or not. It will be evident in the quality of your work and how you prioritize tasks.

Another client knew that we really cared about her and her business. She wrote:

I'm so grateful a friend recommended Karen's virtual assistant business. Karen's been fun and easy to work with. She gets things done so quickly and her attention to detail means I'm not spending as much time editing and correcting mistakes as I used to with my former VA. I'm spending more time doing what I'm good at and enjoying my business more! I highly recommend her! —Melody LeBaron, Founder, Transforming Space

- **E – Excellence:** In Chapter Six, you discovered that you have so many assets. Perfect your gifts, talents, and skills by doing your absolute best work for your clients. Make going an extra mile a core value in your business. Make your clients feel like they have the best deal in the planet, and like working with you is a gift from Heaven, for indeed it is! Make your clients feel like you are the world's greatest hidden secret and they were lucky to discover you. Doing your absolute best work, being thorough, over-delivering on your promises, beating deadlines, and going above and beyond to exceed your client's expectations will make your clients want to hoard you for themselves, and this will guarantee a long-term relationship. No one willingly lets go of a good thing.

When you do excellent work, your clients will have something to say about it, such as our client, Manish:

Working with Karen and her team has been fantastic. Before we brought her on, our response time was horrible—sometimes many days or over a week. And now, our customers often get responses within eight hours. It's really made a difference in our business. It's lowered our refund rates, and it's improved our customer satisfaction. Karen always goes above and beyond to make sure my customers are happy, and she is a pleasure to work with. —Manish Punjabi, Marketing Manager, Coffee Shop Millionaire

I've shared these testimonials to show you why creating your core values and developing a strategy on how to live them out is important. If you are intentional about the kind of business that you want to create, it will have a positive impact on your clients.

When I requested that my clients send me testimonials, I was pleasantly surprised to find that their feedback reflected our business core values. This meant that our core values were clear in the way we performed our work and served our clients. They were able to see that we were trustworthy and reliable, set high standards of excellence, and had impeccable work ethics—we did outstanding work and we actually cared for them and the success of their businesses.

Refer to your answers from the "Business Assessment" exercise in Chapter Five. Look at the answers that identified your business core values. These are the values that you want your clients to know you stand for as you interact with them.

Another way of nourishing your business is by asking for feedback. Every several months, send a check-in email to your clients to find out how they are doing, and to ask if there are any areas for which they would like to see improvement. This will help you get a sense for what you need to improve as well as insight on the areas that you excel in. You can set a quarterly reminder on your calendar to check in with your clients.

Another thing that you could do is to ask for testimonials. After working with your clients for a few months, you can ask them to write you a testimonial. Most clients are more than happy to write you one.

Please note that feedback is different from testimonials. Feedback is more of an assessment of your services, whereas a testimonial is like an endorsement of your services. So, if you don't have a good relationship with a client, you might not want to ask for a testimonial from them, but you should ask for feedback so that you can identify the areas you need to work on to improve your relationship and your services.

Ask for referrals. Reach out to the clients that you've developed a good relationship with and who've given you both positive feedback and testimonials, and ask them to refer you to other business owners who may be in need of your services.

Just a word of advice though: In my experience, some (not all) of the clients that I had the best relationships with and who loved my work the most were the ones who were unwilling to send me referrals. They wanted to keep me to themselves. While it was a great compliment—they didn't want to share me with anyone—it wasn't in my best interest. They believed that they would not receive the same quality work if they sent more clients my way. However, when our business relationships ended for one reason or another, they were more than glad to send me referrals.

When you create a business, especially when you feel called to it, have reverence for the whole process. Be sure to take care of your business. Be a good steward of your business. When you have been entrusted with a divine assignment, it's important that you take ownership of the responsibility, honor it, and execute with excellence.

In the next chapter, we will focus on embracing and enjoying the journey of mompreneurship.

CHAPTER 10
EMBRACE AND ENJOY

"We have a choice every day regarding the attitude we embrace for that day."
—*Charles Swindoll*

Here, you will learn tips and practices to adopt to help you embrace and enjoy your new journey without stress, overwhelm, or burnout.

You are a business owner! You have clients; they are keeping you busy! And your bank account is proof that you actually own a business, not a hobby! You are getting paid for the excellent work that you do. Hard to believe, right? Congratulations! I am so proud of you!

I want you to embrace your identity as a business owner and the adventurous growth journey that comes with it. Enjoy the roller coaster ride, with its exhilarating highs and stomach-churning lows. At the end of it all, it will be worth every single moment! And if you were asked if you would do it all over again, I know your answer would be a resounding, "Yes!"

EMBRACE

It's very important that you remember that you are a business owner. You are not an employee. You've started your business to solve a problem. You are a servant, delivering a valuable service to your clients. Therefore, embrace who you are and walk in that identity.

I have worked with many virtual assistants who, although they were self-employed business owners, operated as though they were still employed by someone else. They thought of their clients as they had their employers. This is a very disempowering place to work from, and not only did it not serve them, it did not serve the client either.

Your clients are not looking to hire an employee. They are looking for a virtual assistant to add value to their business. They want a virtual assistant who solves problems and reduces their workload. They are looking for a VA who will make a contribution to the success of their business. They are searching for a VA who brings expertise to the table, which means that you should be taking the lead on bringing solutions to the client, rather than waiting for the client to micromanage you or show you what to do all the time.

I want you to start on the right footing from the beginning. I want you to shift your mindset. Every day, remind yourself that you are a business owner just like your client. You are equals. They may have been in business longer than you have, but you are both business owners. Consider your relationship as a partnership or collaboration. You are working together towards accomplishing defined goals.

When you function in your identity as a business owner, your clients will view you as an expert. You will command respect as an equal partner. You will take pride and ownership your role. You will have the confidence to charge fees that reflect the value and contribution that you bring.

As a new business owner, you will need to learn many things. Not only will you need to improve your skills as a virtual assistant, you will also need to learn the various aspects of running a business. Therefore, be willing to learn, to grow, and to stretch out of your comfort zone.

As you identify your clients' dynamic needs, take the initiative to learn. Google will be your best friend. There are many free articles, blogs, YouTube videos, ebooks, and e-courses that you can benefit from. Take advantage of these resources. As your business continues to grow, invest in yourself by buying books, taking paid online trainings and courses, and attending workshops. All the knowledge that you gain will help you add even more value to your clients and validate the higher prices that you will charge your clients in time.

Be willing to grow not only in your business but also in your personal and family life. Invest in your spiritual, mental, emotional, and physical wellbeing. The healthier and more whole you are, the better a business owner you will be. After all, your business is an extension of you! Your business will be as healthy as you are.

In order for you to grow, you will have to be comfortable with being uncomfortable. Growth requires that we stretch out of our comfort zones. Sometimes it requires doing things that we're afraid of doing, or that are even painful. Sometimes it requires having difficult conversations. Sometimes it forces us to humbly own up to our mistakes and apologize to our clients or team members. Whatever form it takes, growth is necessary for our continual health. Embrace growth.

I recall when my business reached a point where our clients' customer service needs were growing beyond my team's capacity to meet them. I had to make a decision to partner with a call center. It was a difficult decision to make because I didn't know how it would work. I had no idea if the call center would deliver what they promised, and I was afraid that my client would decide to find a different company that had the capacity to manage their increasing customer-support needs. I was scared. But I knew that the only way to increase our capacity so that we could support our clients well was to take a leap of faith and trust that the call center would come through. And four years down the road, we continue to enjoy a mutually beneficial relationship that's founded on mutual trust and respect. This decision alone catapulted my business to a level that I had never dreamed of. Our revenue doubled instantly, and we were able to serve the clients we had at that time as well as our new clients in a much bigger way than we ever could have in the past.

Had I chosen not to take the risk, had I chosen to cower in fear, we would still be playing small, at a level that was much lower than what was possible for us. With this growth in our capacity, we've had to learn many new things and adjust our operations accordingly. But every single learning moment and adjustment has been worth the effort.

Another way to grow is to glean from your clients. Take the initiative to learn about your clients' businesses: how they operate, how they market, how they plan for the future, and how they serve their clients. This is practical, hands-on learning that you get free of charge as you work with your clients. There is so much that you can learn! Be curious. Ask questions. Your clients will be glad to share the information with you so that you can understand their business, which will in turn help you serve them better. And as you learn from your clients, apply the strategies or techniques that are applicable to your business.

As I shared at the beginning of this book, my first client was an author and a book publisher. I can trace my inspiration to write this book back to her. As I served her and learned more about her business, the seed to write my own book was sown. Almost ten years later, here I am writing the book.

Also, I'm in the process of getting certified as a coach. I strongly believe that one of my clients who is a business coach was divinely put in my path so that I could learn what I needed in order to walk my destiny's path. While I served her as a virtual assistant, unbeknownst to her and even to me at the time, she was unveiling to me the behind-the-scenes workings of her coaching business so that I could glean and learn. I believe that God was preparing me for my future. I didn't know then that I would become a coach, but here I am now, training and coaching clients on how to start a VA business. So, as you embrace your business, be curious and apply what you learn not only to your clients' businesses, but to yours as well.

ENJOY

Two years after I started my business at a time when I was really seeking God and trying to align every part of my life with His will and purpose for my life, I had an epiphany! I thought to myself, in a moment of feeling "godly" (I laugh at myself as I recall this), that I would surrender my business to God so He could take charge and be in control of it. So, I declared to Him that I was surrendering my business to Him and asked Him to have His way in it. And to my utter surprise, He said to me that my business had always been His from the beginning. However, I had taken the driver's seat, which was not mine but His!

I got off my holy high horse in humility and took my rightful place, which was the passenger seat. He told me that He was the Owner, and He was the One that directs the business. I was the manager, and my role was to serve and run the operations of the business. He said that He was the One who brought in clients and directed and defined the vision and mission of the business. My job was to steward it.

That revelation was a life-changing event for me and my business. That was the last day that I worried about where or how to find clients. It was not my job. Never again did I worry about money, whether there was enough to pay myself, my team, and the business expenses. It wasn't my job. God was the Provider.

I share my story to inspire you to find your unique way of enjoying your business. For me, surrendering my business to God released me from stressing and worrying about all the decisions that needed to be made. I trust God to lead and direct how we run the business. He has faithfully done so. It's a freeing and liberating way of being. I truly enjoy my business and I trust that you will enjoy yours too.

Giving up control of my business to God has helped me relax and enjoy my business. I rarely stress about money. I have learned to trust God, and over and over again He has remained true to His Word. Whenever I start to worry about money, I remind myself that I am out of my position. I'm seated in the driver's seat, not my rightful seat—the passenger seat.

My business has reminded me many times of a miraculous story in the Bible about a widow with two sons (I am a single mother with two sons) who, in desperation to save her sons from being sold as slaves to pay off her dead husband's debt, called on a prophet for help. The prophet performed a miracle using a small jar of oil. The mother was able to fill up many jars with oil, sell them, pay off the debt, and have enough for her family. God miraculously has filled and continues to fill my jar of oil through my business.

I have found that when you and your business are in alignment with God, then everything else naturally flows with ease.

God also gave me His vision for my business, which was first and foremost to be a conduit for His financial provision for me and my kids and for all my team members, including the call center. My business also expresses God's love through how we serve our clients—our core values are reflections of God's nature. We also make monthly contributions to specific ministries and causes that advance His Kingdom. We pray during our team meetings, and we pray over our clients, our team members, and the business in general.

Here are some practical tips to help you avoid stress, overwhelm, and burnout.

- **Self-Care** – Take care of yourself. Your well being should be your priority. Set aside time every day to do at least one thing that nurtures you spiritually, emotionally, physically, and mentally.

  I sleep for seven to eight hours every day, and I walk for forty-five minutes, five days a week. I journal, pray, or read the Bible daily. I constantly tweak my food intake as I identify foods that work best with my body and eliminate those that are not beneficial. I enjoy watching shows and movies with my kids, going on retreats, reading books, hiking, spending fun times with friends, and visiting new places.

What do you like to do? Schedule it on your calendar and make your self-care a priority.

- **Manage Your Time** – List your personal, family, and business priorities. Create a master to-do list, then assign deadlines or due dates to each item. Add these tasks into your calendar and set reminders.

I use both a manual planner and Google Calendar. I use the last week of every month to plan for the upcoming month. I schedule all the known and recurring activities on both calendars. Then, each week I add any new activities as they come. Every morning, I create a task list for the day.

Being a stay-at-home mom and businesswoman will require that you really master this skill so that you are able to balance your family and work time. A great book to read is *The 7 Habits of Highly Effective People* by Stephen R. Covey. He talks about setting your priorities in this order: important and urgent, important and not urgent, not important and urgent, and lastly not important and not urgent. The activities listed under "important and urgent" take priority over all other tasks. "Not important and not urgent" tasks could potentially be removed from your tasks list. They could be assigned to someone else or may not need to be done at all.

It's important to decide what time will be your official family time and which will be your official work time. Your work hours would ideally be when you can work uninterrupted for several hours at a stretch. Honor these times as much as possible and keep distractions at bay during your work hours—blocks of uninterrupted time allow you to be super-focused and productive.

Set reasonable deadlines with your clients. Make sure that your deadlines are in alignment with your personal and family needs as well.

- **Set Boundaries** – Learn to say no. Don't work on weekends if those are not your official hours. Don't take on more work than you can handle if you know it will hurt your family. Learn to negotiate deadlines when necessary to avoid conflicts with your family schedule. Your clients will respect your work hours if you communicate them clearly. However, if you're always available at your client's whims, they will keep expecting you to always be at their beck and call. So make sure that you set clear boundaries right from the beginning of your relationship.

Once in a while your client may ask you to work during your "off" hours. Be willing to accommodate your client's request if something very important is at stake. For instance, if your client is launching a new product and unexpected delays require that you work during your "off" hours in order to meet the deadline, then accommodating this request will communicate to her that you have her back. It will strengthen your relationship with your client, who will feel that you are truly invested in the success of their business. However, let such requests be the exception, not the norm.

If you plan well in advance with your clients, you will be able to complete your tasks on time without having to compromise your family's time. This will also help you eliminate stress, overwhelm, and burnout.

- **Celebrate Your Accomplishments** – Reward yourself when you succeed. When you achieve your goals or hit any milestones that you have set for yourself, go out and celebrate. Do something to commemorate it. It will motivate you to keep pursuing your goals and your dreams.

- **Plan Your Finances** – Money is one of the greatest sources of stress in our lives. Taking charge of how you spend and invest your money will relieve you of financial stress, which is a critical part of self-care. A great resource you could consider looking into is the <u>Financial Peace University</u> workshop by Dave Ramsey. I attended this training a few years ago, and the simple strategies taught in the program helped me get out of debt and armed me with tools and strategies for how to invest my money.

- **Gather a Support System** – Create a support system to encourage you and build you up in your personal, family, and business lives. Invest your time and energy in nourishing your relationships with your family, friends, and team. Join some of the VA networking groups I recommended in Chapter Eight. These are great virtual support systems where you can be a part of groups with like-minded people who share your interests. You could join a local Moms of Preschoolers group (MOPs), a single moms' community group, a book club, or a hiking meetup group. There are many community groups out there. Join a few that resonate with you. It's a healthy way to care for yourself. We all need the support of the people around us because we are social beings created for community.

I hope you carve out time to embrace and enjoy your kids. I know when they are little it's a lot easier, especially if they are mellow, quiet, and laid-back. As they grow older and start challenging your parenting, it may be difficult to enjoy the motherhood journey. The way to overcoming this challenge is to be intentional about it. Focus on who they are—their true identity—and invest time to nurture your relationship with your kids more as they grow older.

The same is true of your business. Be intentional about embracing and enjoying your journey as a new business owner. After all, your VA business is your baby. Apply all the tips and strategies that I have shared in this chapter and adopt any others that resonate with you or align with your personality and values. Slow down, smell the coffee, and savor your business.

We have come to the end of this chapter. If you're wondering what's coming next, well, flip the page to find out! I promise you'll enjoy it.

CHAPTER 11
D — DREAM AND GROW

*"The future belongs to those who
believe in the beauty of their dreams."*
—*Eleanor Roosevelt*

I am so proud of you for getting to the last step of the ALIGNED process! If you're working on the steps as you read this book, your business will now be up and running. The first five steps helped you get your business started, and the last three are here to help you sustain it. I like to think of these last three steps as the oil that keep the business running smoothly.

By the time you get to this stage in your business in real life, you should be enjoying the luxury of raising your own kids and spending quality time with your family while making great money running your business. You should be able to afford the life that you always dreamed of. You are doing it! You are living it!

Hard as it may be to imagine, a day will come when you will start to get bored. What you are doing right now that's so exhilarating *will* get old. Something deep inside of you will start wanting more. You will no longer be satisfied with where you are and what you're doing. You will want more for yourself and for your family. When this happens, don't be alarmed. Just know that it's normal. It's part of your metamorphosis. We were created to continuously grow, change, move, be transformed. We're not meant to stay in the same place, doing the same thing, forever. As women, we're designed to keep birthing new things (kids, ideas, businesses, causes, missions, you name it). We were born to create, and to nurture what we birth.

So when you start getting bored and restless and almost ready to shut down your business, know that it's time to start dreaming again. It's time to get pregnant with new dreams and ideas. It's time to have new visions. Allow yourself the time to dream, to imagine, to visualize your next thing. Whether it's in your personal life, family, or business, allow yourself to be comfortable in this very uncomfortable season. Sometimes it takes a short time to discover your next thing; other times it takes years. I encourage you to just keep doing what you already do: Push past the boredom and restlessness and keep putting one foot in front of the other. Do not make any drastic decisions in this transition season. Be slow in making major, life-changing decisions until you are close to the end or are out of this restless period. Be patient with yourself. Ideas may not be free flowing, especially if you feel on edge. Try as much as possible to be relaxed and allow your soul to be in a place of rest. It's only when you are at rest that new dreams and visions start to flow effortlessly.

Keep a journal handy all the time. Write down all your ideas, thoughts, and dreams as they come. You'll be so happy that you did when you look back and see how your ideas got more fleshed-out and refined over time.

Since I started my business, I've experienced this feeling twice. The first time this happened was when I started yearning to do more than just the work I did in my business. I started longing to serve at my church to a greater degree, but I was clueless as to what I could possibly do, since it was a small church and much of its activities were confined to Sundays. I wanted to give more time toward a cause that I believed in. Then the idea to look for single mothers to support popped into my head. I joined a meetup group for a short period of time, and eventually I ended up partnering with its founder to help start a non-profit organization called Thrive Single Moms that's dedicated to engaging, equipping, and empowering single mothers.

I had been a single mother for six years and I had experienced and overcome many of the challenges and much of the emotional pain that came with separation and child custody negotiations. I was passionate about giving hope, encouragement, and support to other single mothers.

So, I made some adjustments in my business. I set up systems and processes and built a strong team to support my new dream of serving single mothers. This meant that I would spend less time on my business to make my new dream a reality. I had to overcome the fear of the unknown. At that time, I was not sure that I could trust my team to run the business without me. I was also afraid if I spent less time on my business, our revenue would go down. None of my fears came true, and I'm glad I trusted my team because they did amazing work. God continued to be in the driver's seat, ensuring that the revenue that we needed to run the business was always generated. I don't know how He did it or does it. It's an ongoing miracle!

You will know when it's time to go to the next level. It will require some planning and courage. Press past your fear of the unknown and take the plunge! Though it may feel painful to get out of your comfort zone, I promise you that you will survive. You will grow; you will go to the next level without regrets. As the famous Nike slogan says, "Just do it!"

Over the years, I have seen many VAs move into one or more of the following areas of specialization. This may not be true for you, but as you start dreaming again, you may want to explore some of these areas. You may find something that resonates with you perfectly, or an idea that triggers other ideas.

- **Writing** – If you're a gifted writer, you may decide to specialize in writing: creative writing, ghost writing, blog writing, ebook writing, copy-writing, technical writing, grant writing, white paper writing, essays, theses or report writing, proofreading, or copyediting. These are potential services that you could specialize in.

- **Tech-savvy VA** – If you're a techy person, you may decide to specialize in technical stuff only. For example: Web design, development, and maintenance; software development; mobile-app development; blog design; online security administration; technical customer service support; Search Engine Optimization; shopping cart and CRM setup; squeeze or landing page set-up; or video and audio creation and editing.

  You could specialize in setting up specific software for your clients. For example: CRMs, helpdesks, virtual classrooms, or membership sites.

- **Graphics Designer** – If you have an artistic touch and graphic design is your skillset, you may choose to only focus on desktop publishing and graphic design. You could decide to specialize in a specific product design: book covers, book layout and design, social media inspirational postcards, business calendars, invitation cards, brochures, journals, or a combination of products.

- **Marketing** – If you're a marketing genius, then you may consider specializing in marketing: email marketing, social media marketing, paid advertising, mobile advertising, press releases, lead generation, direct mail marketing, offline marketing, affiliate marketing, search engine optimization and marketing, or product launches.

Other areas of specialization that you may want to consider, depending on your unique skillset, are: paralegal services, tax services, payroll services, accounting and/or bookkeeping services, medical transcription services, voice-over services, podcast services, recruitment services, customer service support, and video and audio transcription services.

Another direction that VAs venture into is online business management. An online business manager, or OBM, oversees the projects, team, and processes in a business. They are in charge of making sure that the business is running smoothly, all systems and processes are in place, and the right team is hired and delivering their services as expected.

The focus of an OBM is management and overseeing operations, while a VA's focus is *doing*—getting tasks done.

If you are interested in learning more about becoming an OBM, look up Tina Forsyth's <u>online business manager training</u>. It's a great certification program. I did the program and got certified as an OBM as part of my business-growth process.

You could also consider increasing your revenue by expanding your capacity to serve more clients by hiring or sub-contracting the services of other VAs. This is called a team-based virtual assistant business. It is a great opportunity to make more money. However, it's important to know that the additional revenue you make will be the net profit after paying your VA team and any related expenses.

In keeping with your own personal, family, and business goals, this business model will align with your core values. There are only so many hours in a day, and one person can only do so much work. Adding more people to your team increases your ability to do more work, which will generate you more revenue.

I took the OBM certification course, at first thinking that that's what was next for me, but I quickly figured that rather than managing other people's businesses, I needed to be my first OBM client. I applied the management skills that I learned into my own business. What I learned helped to propel my business to the next level—I was able to create systems and processes, and hire a team of virtual assistants and later a call center. Making the decision to take the OBM certification course and applying the knowledge I acquired was a game changer for my business.

A year or two later, with systems, processes, and a team in place, I found myself in my second season of restlessness. I had made myself almost obsolete in my business, and it was then that I ventured into doing the non-profit work for the single mothers' organization that I mentioned earlier.

Even writing this book was preceded by a period of boredom and restlessness. From these examples, I hope you can see that it never ends. As we commit to our own personal growth, we will start to notice a pattern. We dream, we manifest our dream, then we get restless. We dream again, manifest our dream again, and then become restless again. That's the way it's supposed to be. We were created to fill this earth and subdue it with the things we bring to life. We are co-creators with God.

The ALIGNED process can be applied to every new thing that you venture into. The first step is to make an assessment of where you are and where you want to go. Trust me: As you morph and grow, so will your family and business. It's important to do an evaluation every few years. Answering the questions in the Chapter Five exercises will help you keep track of where you are.

The next step is to "Look Within To Find Your Assets." You will be amazed at how many more gems (gifts, talents, and more) you have locked inside you, just waiting to be discovered and excavated.

The third step is where you take in the information you gathered in the first two steps above. "Ingest and Integrate" your findings and set goals that align with your values.

Then go and get your next venture accomplished! That's step number four in the ALIGNED process: G – Go! Get Your Business Started! Whatever it is that you want to embark on, do your research, take the courses or classes that you need, and just do it!

Then follow the last three steps to maintain and sustain what you create. The last three steps, just to remind you, are: N – Nurture What You Create; E – Embrace and Enjoy your new journey, then lather, rinse and repeat; and D – Dream and Grow again.

It will take courage, but know that you have what it takes. Tom Fitzgerald said it perfectly, "If you can dream it, you can do it." You were born to create, to breathe new life, and to nurture what you've created. Your next idea may be in something totally new. It may not necessarily be anything I have mentioned here. That's okay. You are on a unique journey here on earth to do what only you can do. So, don't limit yourself or God. Whatever it is, pursue it!

But first, I must warn you about dream killers.

CHAPTER 12
DREAM KILLERS

"The brave man is not he who does not feel afraid,
but he who conquers that fear."
—Nelson Mandela

We are now drawing close to the end of this book. Before I finish, I must warn you about dream killers. I want to go a little deeper to add on to what I briefly mentioned in Chapter One. I want to prepare you: Expect opposition. Expect resistance. Expect conflict. The moment you decide to go forward and start your virtual assistant business, you will experience all kinds of forces that will try to pull you away from pursuing your dream.

Your dream will be put to the test immediately. It's almost as though it has to go through an authenticity test. Is it a credible dream? Is it a valid dream? How much resistance can your dream withstand? How much opposition can it take? Will it really manifest?

Every time I have made a major life-changing decision or pursued my dreams, right along with the decision came immense inner turmoil in the form of paralyzing fears, self-defeating thoughts, and debilitating insecurities.

I tell you this not to scare you, but to prepare you so that when it happens, you can resolve to push through every obstacle in whatever form it comes until you make your dream a reality.

As soon as you decide to start your virtual assistant business, you will experience exhilarating joy and excitement just thinking of what's possible for your future. In the same breath you will be a nervous wreck, worried sick about failing or succeeding, afraid of losing friends, and fearful of criticism and judgment. Crazy, right? Yes! I've been down that road many times.

- **Fear** – If there's one thing that will stop you dead in your tracks, it is fear. Fear will literally paralyze you and keep you stuck if you allow it to. You can expect an onslaught of fearful thoughts to bombard your mind when you decide to embark on this journey. Fear will bring confusion in your mind. Now that you've read this book, you have the exact steps to what you need to do and how you need to get started. But I promise you, as soon as you decide you are ready to start, your dream's enemy, fear, will pay you a visit, and if you entertain her long enough, she will talk you out of your dream. When she knocks at your door, be sure that she will find an excited, confident you, ready to take on the world. If you're not careful, she will leave you afraid, full of doubt, confused, and with no self-esteem at all. So, please do not entertain fear.

I make it sound easy, but it's not. That's why I'm preparing you in advance to push past the fear. The acronym "FEAR" stands for False Expectations Appearing Real, and it really sums it up. Fear is a false imagination of what you expect to happen in the future without having any tangible evidence or proof to support that expectation. So, fear is only in the mind. It is not real.

As you get ready to start your business, pay close attention to your thoughts and identify your fears. Ask yourself, *What am I really afraid of and why?* And as you list your fears, for each one that you write down, ask yourself, *Is there any truth to this? Is this FEAR or is it a valid concern?* If it's FEAR, then ignore it and keep pushing forward. If it's a valid concern, ask yourself, *How can I mitigate this fear? What do I need to do to minimize or nullify it?* Do you need support? Do you need more information? When you look fear straight in the face, it cowers and shrinks.

As you make major decisions in your life, you can be sure that you won't always be 100 percent confident or fearless. Many times you will be shaking in your boots as you go after the things you want in your life and in your business. But if you don't take action, you will find yourself stuck and unable to make progress.

So, determine to make your dream come true in spite of the fear you face. Make a pact with yourself in advance that you will accomplish your goals no matter what, with God's help. It will call for courage. Courage is not the absence of fear, it's doing what you need to do despite being afraid.

When my kids first discovered that I didn't know how to swim because I was afraid of drowning, they pointed their tiny fingers at me one summer afternoon and shouted, "Mommy, face your fear!" Where did my four- and six-year-old boys learn such great advice? I don't know. Well, I took their counsel and signed up for swimming classes. I won't say I am a great swimmer or that I enjoy it, but I did get over my fear of drowning! And my kids were very proud of me. So, if you're afraid, imagine my kids with little serious faces, pointing tiny fingers and instructing you: "Face your fear!" If taking a class, like I had to, is what you have to do, then do it!

Another way of conquering fear is by following a plan. Having a plan makes it easy because you don't have to figure things out on your own. I have given you a plan to follow—the ALIGNED process. You know what you need to do, so you don't have any reason or excuse not to start your business. Follow the steps and just do it!

Sometimes the feelings of fear can be very unpleasant, overwhelming, and extremely uncomfortable. Push past the fear by focusing on the big picture. Remind yourself why you wanted to start your business in the first place. You wanted freedom and flexibility to make the money you need to afford the lifestyle that you desired for your family. You wanted to be present and available for your family. You wanted to be the best mom and/or spouse that you could be. Let your "big why" inspire you to push past your fear.

Prayer works for me. When I am afraid, I pray. I find that when I release my fear to God, my faith increases. I start believing that I am capable and competent, and with God's help, I know that everything is possible. Prayer helps me shift my perspective. When I trust God with the outcome of my efforts, I know that in the end everything will be just as it should. It's very freeing.

I encourage you to stay the course. Sit through the feelings of discomfort and know that they will wear off if you don't give up. You will be pleasantly surprised to discover that what we fear might happen usually never does. It's just False Evidence Appearing Real (but it's *not* real).

- **Naysayers** – Not everyone will be happy about your dream, so be careful about who you share it with. Even your closest family and friends may not necessarily support you or your dream. They will share their worries, concerns, doubts, and fears. Some of these will be legitimate feedback, but some may be projections of their own fears and insecurities. Some may tell you outright that you will not succeed. So be ready for that.

When I first shared my dream of starting a virtual assistant business with a close friend, I was discouraged when he told me that I didn't have the personality of a business owner and that at best I could only give stuff away for free because I was incapable of selling anything to anyone. To say that I was crushed and demoralized is an understatement, but I learned that I couldn't rely on people to make my dreams come true. So I resolved to start my business anyway. And to my utter surprise, I got my first client within just a few weeks of registering my business!

- **Complacency** – This is another obstacle that will threaten to abort your dream. Please don't settle for where you are. Don't allow your dream to be snatched away by complacency. Change is uncomfortable, but become comfortable with being uncomfortable. Nothing is ever guaranteed or certain in the business world or in life, and change is inevitable. Change is happening whether we like it or not, so welcome it. Change weeds out complacency. Change forces us to make adjustments and to grow. Growth is usually painful, but it's always worth it.

  Complacency is a form of inertia. Newton's first law states that "an object will remain at rest or move at a constant speed in a straight line unless it is acted on by an unbalanced force." This is true of us as human beings as well. When we get comfortable with the status quo, we stunt our growth and potential. Change, discomfort, growth, and pain are the forces that get us out of our state of inertia. When you persevere through the discomfort and the pain that is necessary to grow, you will be so glad that you did! I promise you!

- **Lack of support** – Starting your business can be a lonely journey. Virtual assistance has gained popularity in the last decade, but there are still many people who have no idea who a virtual assistant is. So don't be surprised to find that no one in your circle knows about virtual assistance, and be prepared to explain over and over again what you do. And even after you've explained it to them, they may still never understand. To this day, my parents and some of my close friends still can't explain what I do to anyone. All they know is that I work from home.

So know that, as much as your close family and friends love you and may want to support you, they may not necessarily be able to do it in a way that's meaningful to you because of their lack of knowledge. Don't be discouraged or disappointed, because not everyone in your close circle of friends and family is supposed to walk this journey with you. Join the support groups I recommended in Chapters Eight and Nine and create a new support system for your business.

- **Insecurities** – If there's one more thing that I can add to this list of dream killers, it would have to be insecurities. Your insecurities will show up when you least expect them to, and at very inconvenient moments. Like right now, as you contemplate taking this huge step of faith to start your business. Your insecurities will come to you in the form of that voice in your head that brings doubt and tears down your self-confidence. The interrogative voice that asks you, *Who do you think you are to start your business? What makes you think you are all that? What makes you think you are smart? Who do you think will pay your bills? What if you fail?* Those questions that make you question your credibility. The questions that make you feel uneasy, unsure, uncertain, and nervous. The questions that make you want to hide in a corner in shame for even daring to think that you were capable of starting your own business.

I'm here to prepare you, because your insecurities *will* show up. When they do, go back to the work you did in Chapters Four, Five, and Six to remind yourself of how amazingly gifted you are and how well equipped you are to start your business. Remind yourself of who you are, of the assets that you possess, and answer every question that causes you to doubt yourself with the truth that you discovered in the work you did in those three chapters.

To wrap up, I want you to know that I believe in you and I'm cheering you on. If I, a single mother of two preteen boys, have done it for ten years now, you can do it too! I was exactly where you are. Just like you, I wanted to be available for my family as much as possible. Life is too short, and children grow so fast. I didn't want to miss out on important moments in their lives. I wanted to be actively involved in raising my boys, yet I also knew that I'm blessed with many gifts, skills, and talents. I wanted to make use of them and make a good income to provide for myself and my family.

I wanted to have a flexible schedule that allowed me to do the things I enjoyed doing with my family with no restrictions on time. I wanted to attend school field trips with my kids when they started school. I wanted to be able to do homework with them after school. I wanted the flexibility to plan my work schedule around my family's needs. I wanted to be able to sleep in if I was up till the wee hours of the morning when my kids were sick.

I wanted to be able to pursue my passions, desires, and hobbies now, rather than after retiring. I wanted to design a life that matched my personality and my values, and supported my purpose in life.

I wanted to have an income that would afford me the lifestyle that I wanted to design for myself and my family. And I know you want the same thing too.

One of my mentors, the late Dr. Myles Munroe, often encouraged his students and mentees to "die empty" by choosing to live on purpose and fulfilling all your dreams so that when you die, you'll have emptied yourself by serving others using the gifts that you were given by your Creator. In short, be a gift to humanity—don't take your unrealized potential and dreams to your grave.

Les Brown says it so profoundly in his quote, "The graveyard is the richest place on earth, because it is here that you will find all the hopes and dreams that were never fulfilled, the books that were never written, the songs that were never sung, the inventions that were never shared, the cures that were never discovered, all because someone was too afraid to take that first step, keep with the problem, or determine to carry out their dream."

Don't be one of those who allow fear to rob humanity of the contribution you were born to make to this world. When confronted by fear, naysayers, insecurities, complacency, or lack of support, choose to keep pushing forward and saying yes to your calling. You were born to make a difference.

CONCLUSION

"You cannot swim for new horizons until you have
courage to lose sight of the shore."
—*William Faulkner*

I am so thrilled and humbled that you stuck with me through the chapters of this book. Thank you. It's been an honor and a privilege to share with you my heart and my journey of starting my virtual assistance business. I hope that you will take all the information in the book and apply it to your own journey. And I look forward to hearing your success story in the coming months.

Just to recap, my ALIGNED process contains the steps that I followed while starting my VA business. Through fumbles, costly mistakes, and many blunders along the way, and by the grace of God, I was able to create a successful business. I designed this process in a systematic way so that you don't have to reinvent the wheel. I eliminated time-consuming, costly, and unnecessary steps so that you have the fastest and easiest way to create your own successful virtual assistant business.

The ALIGNED process I outlined in the book took you through the first three foundational steps, where you did an initial assessment to get clear about your goals; a thorough self-exploration that helped you discover who you are and find your skills, talents, strengths and weaknesses, love languages, personality, temperament, and core values, all of which make you unique and special. You then integrated your self-discovery results with your vision, goals, and core values.

In the fourth step, you learned the detailed steps involved in starting and running a virtual assistant business that is in alignment with your vision, core values, and goals. You got strategies in the fifth step to help you nurture and sustain your business and learned tips to eliminate stress, overwhelm, and burnout so that you can enjoy serving your clients from a place of authenticity, ease, and enjoyment.

You also learned to recognize the opportunities available for growth and expansion to inspire you to keep dreaming and growing in the sixth step. And finally, now you know that you can replicate the ALIGNED process for every new dream you want to realize.

I prepared you so that you would be aware of the obstacles to expect and how to overcome them.

In starting your business, you will get to live the life that you've dreamed about. You will be able to spend quality time with you family as you desire. You will model for your kids how to dream big and to chase after the things we want without giving up. You will be an inspiration to your family and friends, and you will definitely make them proud. And most of all, you will make the difference you were created to make by serving your clients and your family.

YOU HAVE EVERYTHING YOU NEED

If you're still unsure about starting your virtual assistant business, look back at the list of tasks and responsibilities of a VA that I outlined in Chapter Eight. Remember, if you can perform 50 percent or more of the tasks listed, then you are ready to start your business. If you are skilled in 25 to 50 percent of the tasks and you are willing to learn more skills, then you qualify as well. If you possess at least four of these soft skills—reliability, attentiveness to details, problem-solving abilities, a willingness to learn, excellent communication skills, and a get-tasks-done attitude—you are also ready to start your VA business. If you lack some of these skills but are willing to learn, then you can start your business as well.

As we come the end of this book, I would like to express my gratitude to you for reading it to the end. It's been my absolute joy and pleasure to share my journey and the ALIGNED process with you. I pray that you feel inspired, motivated, and empowered to take action and make your dream come true. If you would like my one-on-one support and accountability to make your vision and dream a reality, please reach out to me by scheduling time on my calendar at: www.stayathomemomsmaking-money.com/explore

Go! Get your business started! I believe in you!

FURTHER READING

- *Boundaries: When to Say Yes, How to Say No to Take Control of Your Life* by Dr. Henry Cloud and Dr. John Townsend

- *Dave Ramsey's Complete Guide to Money* by Dave Ramsey

- *Maximizing Your Potential: The Keys to Dying Empty* by Myles Munroe

- *Strengths Finder 2.0* by Tom Rath

- *The 5 Love Languages: The Secrets to Love That Lasts* by Gary Chapman

- *The 7 Habits of Highly Effective People: Powerful Lessons in Personal Change* by Stephen R. Covey

- *The Power of Habit: Why We Do What We Do in Life and Business* by Charles Duhigg

- *The Purpose Driven Life: What on Earth Am I Here For?* By Rick Warren

ACKNOWLEDGMENTS

My deepest gratitude goes to my sons, David and Charles, for being my biggest fans, for your heartfelt prayers, support, and encouragement, and for always wishing me success in everything that I do. I hope this book-writing journey has been an inspiration to you.

I want to thank Dad from the bottom of my heart for inspiring me to reach for my greatest potential and to never give up. My deep gratitude goes to Mom for supporting my dreams and always believing in me. I would not be where I am today without you two.

Words cannot express the depth of my gratitude toward my sister, Rose, for running my business single-handed and enabling me to focus on writing this book. It could not exist without you.

Heartfelt and deep thanks to my dear sister and friend, Sophie, for your unshakable belief in me, your unfaltering support, constant encouragement, and feedback. Thanks for walking alongside me every step of my journey to becoming an author.

My sincerest gratitude to my sister, Lydiah, my cousin, Dan, and to my friends Dinah, Vero, and Angela for taking the valuable time to review my initial draft and give me honest feedback. Your fingerprints are all over this book.

Many thanks to my sister, Maggie, and to my friends Gladi, Wilcenia, and my Thrive Single Moms family for holding me accountable by keeping track of my progress. Thank you for your words of encouragement, support, and prayers.

Special thanks to Anne Palmer, my dear friend and client for modeling what living in true alignment with your values, gifts, and purpose looks like. Your impact is evident in this book.

I appreciate Angela Lauria and her team for being the midwives that helped deliver this baby. You were an answer to my prayers. Thank you for the significant part you've played in creating this book and helping me fulfill my calling.

Last but not least, I'm grateful to God for planting within me the desire to write this book and for surrounding me with the support team that I needed to bring it to fruition. Thank You for entrusting me with this work. May it bring You honor and glory.

ABOUT THE AUTHOR

Karen Kamenwa is the founder of Royal Online Business Solutions, a virtual assistant company. She has spent the last ten years mastering the art of running a successful business while raising her two sons as a stay-at-home single mother. She holds a bachelor's degree in Design, is a certified online business manager, has completed CEO Business School, and awaits the receipt of her Integrative Wellness Life Coaching certification.

Karen began her entrepreneurial journey at the age of eighteen when she started her first tutoring business. Over the years, she continued to build her business acumen through her work experience in large multinational organizations such as British American Tobacco, the parent company of Reynolds American; and PricewaterhouseCoopers. Along with her continued education, trainings, and years of experience serving diverse and dynamic small business owners and online enterprises, Karen is considered an expert in the virtual assistant industry.

Karen's desire to earn a living without sacrificing quality time with her children was the catalyst for starting her business. She built a business that not only provides services to its clients and financially sustains her family and its workers, but also enables her to spend time with her family, volunteer at her church and in her local community, and invest her resources in causes that she believes in. In short, she has designed a life of purpose that she enjoys and is proud of.

With her experience, knowledge, and expertise, she helps mothers start virtual assistant businesses so that they can have financial freedom and flexibility to design lives they love, enjoy, and can afford without compromising quality time with their families.

When she is not working on her business, she volunteers at Thrive Single Moms, a non-profit organization, as the Training & Curriculum Development Director, and hosts a small group Bible study at her home.

Karen lives in California with her two wonderful sons. She enjoys supporting and empowering single mothers, reading, hiking, and spending time and having fun with family and friends. On the weekend, she is often found on the sidelines of sports fields cheering her athletic sons.

Website: www.stayathomemomsmakingmoney.com
Email: wecare@stayathomemomsmakingmoney.com
Facebook: www.facebook.com/karen.kamenwa.3

THANK YOU

I sincerely hope my book has inspired and encouraged you to step out and live your best life. Don't let anything stop you from making your dream a reality. Your time is now!

I know we covered a lot of material in this book. That is why I created e-copies of all the exercises in the book for you to download and print for easy use. This is my simple way to express my heartfelt gratitude and to serve you further so that you have everything you need to take your life to the next level.

Visit my website at: www.stayathomemomsmakingmoney.com/ book-worksheets to download free copies of all the exercises in this book. If you have any questions, don't hesitate to email me at: wecare@stayathomemomsmak- ingmoney.com.

Love and blessings,

Karen Kamenwa

Printed in Great Britain
by Amazon

57877612R00129